GOD, SEX,
THE UNIVERSE
AND ALL THAT

A Lion Book
an imprint of
Lion Hudson plc
Mayfield House, 256 Banbury Road,
Oxford OX2 7DH, England
www.lionhudson.com

ISBN 0 7459 5182 1
ISBN 978 0 7459 5182 9

First edition 2006
10 9 8 7 6 5 4 3 2 1 0

Picture acknowledgments
p. 109 © Getty Images Ltd
p. 122© EMPICS/AP

Text acknowledgments
Scripture quotations are taken from the Holy Bible, New
International Version, copyright © 1973, 1978, 1984
International Bible Society. Used by permission of
Zondervan and Hodder and Stoughton Limited. All rights
reserved.

A catalogue record for this book is available
from the British Library

Printed and bound in the UK by Cox and Wyman Ltd

The text paper used in this book has been made from
wood independently certified as having come from
sustainable forests.

GOD, SEX,
THE UNIVERSE
AND ALL THAT

Roy McCloughry

LION

*For
Lauren,
Lizzie
and Joanna
with love*

Contents

A torch, a rug and a starry night

1

To read this book, you will first need a torch, a rug and a starry night.

Take the torch and use it to find a place away from the light pollution of the city, a place where you can actually see stars. For some of you, this might take some time. Lay the rug on the ground, switch off the torch and let your eyes get properly adjusted until you can see the stars.

You may feel tempted to feel stupid at this point. After all, this is only the first page of the book and you might be asking whether they are all like this. Fear not. This is a one off. It has one purpose. To restore your sense of awe. You may have had a difficult day. Let it go. Live with the stars for a few moments. You share the universe with them and they have something to teach both you and me. They may be unfamiliar to you or you may know them like the back of your hand but I hope you can get lost in them for a while and appreciate their beauty again. They are both art and science combined on a cosmic scale.

We live in a society that has lost its sense of awe. There are, of course, places around the world which can stimulate it again. I remember visiting the Grand Canyon in the US. Parking in a forest, I asked the nearest person where the Grand Canyon was. 'Just down that path,' he said. Walking through the bushes, I came to a clearing and there was the most amazing sight. Below me was a huge chasm carved through the Colorado rock over a period of 2 million years. It is about 277 miles long, up to eighteen miles wide, and a mile deep. The tourist brochures called it 'awe-inspiring' and it was. I could not believe that any person could resist being moved by its scale and beauty.

The same happens for some people when they visit the great cathedrals around the world, which were built in the Middle Ages. The scale of these buildings, the beauty of the craftsmanship and the attention to detail cause us to reflect on the motivations of the stonemasons, carpenters and painters who often spent their whole lives working on one project, built 'to the glory of God'.

> **He who can no longer pause to wonder and stand rapt in awe, is as good as dead; his eyes are closed.**
> *Albert Einstein*

In our own sophisticated modern society, the decline of awe has left a black hole. It has been replaced by an obsession with technological advances that have often indulged our sense of self-importance. So recovering our sense of awe is the first step in any spiritual journey. Without it, we cannot make sense of our lives, or indeed this book.

A throwaway universe

In the story of creation, written in the first few chapters of the Bible, the stars only merit a throwaway line: 'He also

made the stars'. Although there are estimated to be
70,000 million million million stars or, more accurately, 70
sextillion (7 followed by 22 zeros), they represent the most
casual act of creation. Something God did in a coffee
break.

Yet those stars are awe inspiring. Poets, painters,
explorers and scientists have come back to them again and
again for inspiration and guidance. It is difficult also to
ignore them, unless of course we can't see them because
of where we live.

> **Two things fill me with constantly
> increasing admiration and awe, the
> longer and more earnestly I reflect
> on them: the starry heavens
> without and the moral law within.**
> *Immanuel Kant*

When we look at any aspect of human life or
experience, we can view it from many different
perspectives. But on this occasion, we look at the stars as
evidence of something that has to be explained. They
confront us with two choices, each an act of faith or belief.
First, we can believe that they are deliberate and creative
acts made by God or secondly, that they are chance
collections of atoms and nothing more. It's not that one
represents belief in an invisible God and the other is 'hard'
scientific evidence, a provable fact. Instead, they are both
acts of faith. Both are responses to the evidence. The
universe is in the dock. You are on the jury. You decide.

Now switch on the torch again and shine it on your hand.
Look closely at it. No person who has ever lived or ever will
live has your fingerprints. Even identical twins don't have the
same fingerprints. You are unique. The FBI may have tens of

thousands of fingerprints on file but they will need the prints from over 6 billion people to get the full set.

The way you think, feel, love and look is impossible to replicate. You are no accident, no surprise to the universe. Instead, you have been made with the same loving care and attention to detail as the stars. In terms of awe you are made on the same scale as the Grand Canyon. You may feel insignificant compared to the stars but you are not and therefore one of the most important starting points in any spiritual journey is to recover your sense of wonder at who you are and how you came to be here. But as we shall see, the problem is whether you can let yourself believe that.

All of us sometimes ask what is life about. I would argue that it is about discovering that we are loved by somebody and both the identity of this person and the quality of that love can, if we allow it, revolutionise our life. But the issue is, how do we respond to that?

I believe that it's worth catching a cold on a starry night to find that out. Now wrap yourself up in the rug, use your torch to find your way home and go to bed.

Tomorrow is another day.

2 Because you're worth it

Who are we under the skin? Does it make any difference whether we view ourselves as a 'chance collection of atoms' or as someone uniquely special and made for a purpose? Certainly, we seem to be fascinated, perhaps even obsessed, with matters of personal identity but give ourselves little time or space to explore who we are in any depth.

Most glossy magazines revolve around superficial issues of personal identity, inviting comparisons with celebrities and the way they look and live. They provide us with cosmetic tips about how to cover up our blemishes or make us seem more beautiful – nothing wrong in that in itself. They let us in on the secrets of great sex – well, most of us are interested in that. They showcase this year's clothes, this year's look, this year's phone... this year's you.

> **The average American woman is 5'4" tall and weighs 140 pounds**
>
> **The average American model is 5'11" tall and weighs 117 pounds**
>
> **Most fashion models are thinner than 98% of American women**
>
> *www.womensissues.about.com*

But at the heart of this enterprise is maintaining the feeling of dissatisfaction and longing. Dissatisfaction with who we are and longing to be what we could become. When standing in the supermarket checkout idly glancing at the front covers of the magazines on display, we read headlines like: 'I lost thirty pounds in two weeks' or 'have perfect skin in one month' or even 'be a better lover – your guide to the perfect orgasm'.

In all of this, we rarely think about how much time the model spent in make-up covering up their spots or that the search for the perfect orgasm might put our lover under so much pressure that our relationship deteriorates. We cannot win at the game that is being played, designed as it is to keep us restless while promising perpetual fulfilment.

Products or people?

It seems that in such a society, we are mere commodities to be traded rather than people to be respected. In a competitive world, we are the stuff of circulation and sales figures. If a company can keep us dissatisfied with our lives, then it is likely that we may buy its products to improve ourselves.

Perhaps we fill in the endless questionnaires about our perfect partner, consult horoscopes about what is going to happen to us or buy books on how to be an instant success.

These tap into some of our deepest longings to find the perfect partner or to be a success in our career but the way being offered, which may help in the short term, is not usually satisfying in the long term. The alternative message, one that this book will put forward, is that we all want to know who we are, what we are here for and where we are going. To find the answers to these questions, we have to be willing to go on a spiritual journey. These are the big questions – the classics – which people have been asking since life began.

We all want to be fulfilled. But if we succumb to the spirit of the age with its easy fixes, we are in danger of never being content with either who we are or what we have, being kept instead in the twilight world of perpetual longing. Many people think that materialism is driven by the desire to accumulate 'things', but I think that it's driven by something far deeper than that – longing.

It is easy, however, especially when young, to be distracted from these questions because of the pace at which we are living our lives. It is a time when the power of ambition may displace, temporarily, the presence of longing even though there is nothing wrong with ambition when it is in its place. Yet those who do not succeed and instead drop out early, sitting on the touchline as a young adult with little hope of 'getting to the top', find that longing feeling becoming an-all-too familiar companion. With that, self-esteem can quickly plummet and then all kinds of problems may emerge as a sign of distress or anger.

The restless heart

> **Thou hast made us for thyself, O Lord, and our hearts are restless until they find their rest in thee.**
> *St Augustine*

So longing can be displaced by success for a time but it never disappears completely and we all need to come to terms with it at some time in our lives. The quotation from St Augustine above suggests that if we are made by God for a relationship with God, then the absence of that relationship will cause us to be restless. Instead of exploring just how much we are loved by God, we spend our lives searching for an alternative. If Augustine is right and there is nothing else in the world that will bring us such a lasting contentment, then life does become suffused with a longing that cannot otherwise be satisfied.

> **I'm not really religious but very spiritual. I give money to this company that manufactures hearing aids on a regular basis. More people should really hear me sing. I have a gift from God.**
> *Christina Aguilera*

It is the difference between being hungry for a meal which comes and being hungry for a meal which does not. The end result, satisfaction or starvation, could not be more different. Yet our society is spiritually starving. It is not that we are 'unspiritual', as we are fascinated by all sorts of spiritual things. From *The X Files* to *Buffy the Vampire Slayer*, our TV ratings betray our fascination with the supernatural. You just need to look at the 'mind, body and spirit' sections in our bookshops to see the wide array of different beliefs and practices represented. We have become a society of seekers. But if longing is a sign that we are searching for God then the issue is, which is the true God and which are the gods that fail? It seems that nothing we are being offered at the checkout at present will satisfy us at this level – not even the offer of 'true' romance.

Yet for many of us life is moving at a fast pace and these

issues can easily be pushed to one side by more pressing concerns. For people in their late teens, for instance, life is often dominated by the pressure of exams and moving in and out of friendships, with all that goes with them. After this, it may be college that occupies us – with little time for anything else. By the time we enter the world of work, we find ourselves accelerating, our world speeding up.

Technology works 24/7 and takes no coffee breaks, and the more we are dependent on it, the more pressure we seemingly find ourselves under. The problem is that we now live with global systems that are characterised by efficiency whereas as humans, although we can be efficient in our work, we cannot keep up with the machines. We were made for communities characterised by intimacy. The more we have to work to the pace set by technological society, the less time we have for people and the more restless we then become. Without loving and affirming relationships that endure, we can find ourselves adrift at sea. In a world of constant change, it is difficult to settle on our true identity. And our society is always ready to sell us something ready made off the shelf, which though it may be shallow may do for the moment.

There was once a billboard advert displayed, paid for by a cosmetics company. It showed a scantily clad beautiful model and written underneath were the words, 'who do you want to be today?' The implication was that by using this company's products, we could change our identity. But underlying this message was a far deeper one. First, that our identity is changeable, as if we could readily be moulded into a different body shape, and second, that we do actually want to be someone different. It seems that these are two of the most basic assumptions underpinning our consumer society today.

By the way... who do *you* want to be today?

Knowing who we are

Of course we are often made aware that we are different people within different settings. I once went to a party with my wife at which there were a few people from her work. When the dancing started, one woman danced passionately and energetically. She was extremely good. My wife was amazed. 'At work,' she said, 'she's as quiet as a mouse. I never even dreamt that she could be like this.'

But one of our problems is that we are so constrained by the roles given to us by society that we are only able to show a small amount of the person we really are.

And yet it can also be true that in not knowing often who we are, we sometimes settle for the person we think others require us to be. We behave in the way in which the group we are in behaves collectively, perhaps smoking, binge drinking or being sexually promiscuous, even though we may feel that it is not the real us.

I remember a girlfriend of mine once asking me what kind of woman I really liked. Caught off guard and not realising the significance of the question, I reeled off a random set of characteristics that unfortunately did not come close to describing who she was. The next time we met she had dressed differently and looked at me expectantly. It was only some time later that I realised that she was attempting to change to fit the description I had given of my ideal woman. It was no wonder that the relationship went downhill from there. As my daughters would tell me now, I had given the wrong answer with a capital W! The right answer would have been to say, 'someone like you'.

So in the midst of all this, how can we begin to think about ourselves differently? It's worth turning back to the Bible here for help. In the story of creation, we read of God making men and women and pronouncing them good. In fact, one of the most astonishing statements ever made about humanity is found in the first chapter of the Bible, telling us that we are made in the 'image of God'.

In some ways, then, I would argue that we are a self-portrait of God. Since God is invisible, however, it's difficult to be exact about this and it is tempting to say that this passage refers to our ability to reason or some other aspect of our humanity. Perhaps. But I think that what it really means is simply that you and I are in some way made like God. Our goodness is tied to the goodness of God and our beauty to the beauty of God.

> **For you created my inmost being;**
> **you knit me together in my**
> **mother's womb. I praise you**
> **because I am fearfully and**
> **wonderfully made; your works are**
> **wonderful, I know that full well.**
> *Psalm 139:13–14*

We may feel bad about ourselves because of things that happen to us in life. We may look at ourselves in the mirror and be dissatisfied with what we see. Of course we have many flaws, both physically and emotionally, but this idea, that we are made in the image of God, means that we should not only treat other people with dignity and respect but we should treat ourselves with self-respect and hold our heads up a little higher. I believe that we were made by God not only lovingly and carefully, but in some fundamental way as an expression of something of who God is.

This idea gives us two things which are both important. First, it gives us status. We suddenly become enormously important. This is very different, however, to self-importance. Self-important people seem to be empty on the inside. Instead, this is importance given to us as a gift. It has nothing to do with us. We just have it. It is a reflection of who God is. We can't avoid it. Of course we may feel insignificant at times but no person can claim a higher status than to have been the model for a self-portrait of God!

Secondly, if we are a self-portrait of God, then it seems to give us a purpose in life. We are here then for a reason because we have been made deliberately. And because of this, it's very difficult to get away from the idea of purpose and design because it is built into us, it's part of our DNA.

Satisfied with our bodies?

I have a friend called John who is a wheelchair user. He is also a vicar in the Church of England, which is often a surprise to people who see him working in his wheelchair, though I'm not sure why. In a book on disability he writes, '... I have never felt the need for healing. I have known that I am loved by God for who I am, as I am. Scripture also tells me that I am "fearfully and wonderfully made". This message has been the one that has affirmed, rather than negated, my disability.'

Now 'fearfully and wonderfully made' is not the kind of language that we use on a daily basis. It is archaic. But nevertheless, if we can get beyond this, we might see the power of this statement, the radicalism of it within the context of the narcissistic society that we live in today.

We live in a world which is trying to package beauty and sell us products that will make us feel better about ourselves. We think that we are buying consumer products but it seems that it is we who are becoming a consumer product.

One of the most extraordinary trends over the last ten years has been the growth of cosmetic surgery. In the United States, since 1997 there has been a 293 per cent increase in cosmetic surgery. When the magazine *Grazia* polled their readers, they found that 50 per cent of them expected to have cosmetic surgery at some point within their lifetime. Cosmetic surgery has now also become entertainment with a marked growth in reality TV shows that revel in before and after makeovers.

One of the most extreme of these was *Cosmetic Surgery Live*, presented by Vanessa Feltz and Jan Adams, the latter a well-known Los Angeles plastic surgeon. This tabloid-style show beamed live pictures of operations into our living rooms from the operating theatres of Los Angeles even though the British Association of Plastic Surgeons labelled the show 'voyeuristic and pornographic'.

> **Plastic surgery and breast implants are fine for people who want that, if it makes them feel better about who they are. But, it makes these people, actors especially, fantasy figures for a fantasy world. Acting is about being real, being honest.**
> *Kate Winslet*

In another development, *Zoo* magazine held a competition with one of the prizes being breast implants for the prizewinner's girlfriend. Under the headline, 'win a boobjob for your girlfriend', men were invited to send in photos of their girlfriends. The winner would be the one who, in the opinion of the judges, most needed a boobjob. She would then be invited to pose for *Zoo* 'when the scars are healed'. It seems that not only are people dissatisfied with their own bodies but it is now becoming acceptable for boyfriends to express their dissatisfaction with their girlfriends' bodies!

Yet we are all aware of the many tragic problems that people have through a distorted self-image and unhappiness about who they are. It can show itself in the form of eating disorders such as anorexia or bulimia, which cause real suffering and are often difficult to treat. When a young woman (and, increasingly, young men) is dangerously underweight but sees herself as fat when looking in the mirror, then her distorted self-image becomes a serious psychological problem that must be treated if she is to survive or at least avoid doing further damage to her body. This dissatisfaction with the body is also present in the form of over-dieting and the seemingly constant obsession with diets. Our consumer society is, of course, willing to pander to this, producing books, products and gurus with their countless diet and fitness videos to help us, and make a healthy profit in the process.

Another aspect of this dissatisfaction is the recent surge of people signing up to join a gym. These gyms are usually expensive and for some a status symbol that is rarely used beyond the initial month or two. But others go the other way, becoming obsessed with exercise and fitness, going far beyond what is needed to live a healthy life, or even to look good.

Through this, plastic surgery has grown in popularity as an attempt to find contentment with one's body image. It is associated with being happier with oneself. There is a double standard at work here, however, since celebrities will often go as far as to lie to deny that they have had plastic surgery. Presumably this is because there remains some residual stigma about it. Yet for some people, it seems to have become something of an addiction.

And yet plastic surgery is seen by others as an

improvement and given a positive gloss because of its use by celebrities. Although there are people who need serious reconstructive surgery, far too many of those who are currently having plastic surgery are doing so as the new active consumers of paid-for beauty. We now see surgery and beauty products as belonging in the same category.

At its heart, cosmetic surgery is the most recent expression of dissatisfaction with what we look like, with many willing to spend considerable amounts of money to change their appearance. But such attitudes are very different to John who, although facing difficulties as a wheelchair user, accepts himself as he is because of knowing what it means to be loved by God as he is now.

Harming ourselves

At the other end of the spectrum from cosmetic surgery is the issue of self-harm. Once again we are beginning to read of celebrities admitting to self-harm or seeing their photographs in tabloid magazines with cuts on their forearms, suggesting that there is another side to their character from the one that they project publicly.

One of the most recent people to reveal that she has self-harmed is the British athlete Kelly Holmes, who won two gold medals in the 2004 Olympics. She became so low from the number of injuries sustained that she began to cut herself with scissors. This went on for two months. She commented, 'I made one cut for every day I'd been injured. With each one I felt I was punishing myself but at the same time, I felt a sense of release that drove me to do it again and again. I knew deep inside that I wouldn't go any further. The whole episode was nothing more than a cry of despair.'

According to professionals working in the field, the trend to self-harm is becoming something of an epidemic. Whether cutting, poisoning or burning themselves in some way, those who self-harm are attempting to express the pain that is felt within. In some instances, they are trying to avoid suicide by harming themselves in a lesser way, a way that they can control. Yet evidence shows that people who self-harm are much more likely to commit suicide than those who don't.

> **An estimated 170,000 people are hospitalised every year in Britain from self-harm, the majority women, comfortably outnumbering cosmetic surgery in-patients.**

But whereas cosmetic surgery is meant to be a positive statement and self-harm a negative one, both are in fact expressions of dissatisfaction with who we are and increasing trends at the beginning of the twenty-first century. Both show that we are using our bodies as a canvas to alter the portraits of ourselves, wanting to add or subtract something. Sometimes, as with self-harm, we even want to slash the canvas. Perhaps in part, it is because we cannot express adequately what we wish to say in words and so we use our bodies to say what we feel and think about ourselves.

The point of this chapter is not to reassure you that everything will be OK if or when you discover that you are made in the image of God. It's very likely that some people who have a religious faith have had plastic surgery and certain that some have also self-harmed. Christians are certainly not exempt from depression or from thinking that they are physically imperfect.

Nevertheless, it remains true that if we have been 'fearfully and wonderfully made', something has to give in the way that we view both ourselves and those around us. Whatever has happened to us in our life that has caused us to doubt, this cannot begin to change unless we come to see ourselves differently. This was what marked the beginning of the 'disability movement' when people like John realised that although they had an impairment, they did not need to see themselves as either victims or powerless. As they began to celebrate their lives and see themselves as contributors to the life of the community rather than passive consumers of its welfare resources, life began to change.

Celebrating who we are

It seems today that our celebrity culture is relatively empty and false. Why is it that so many celebrities seem to be dissatisfied with their lives and take drugs, get drunk and frequently change their partners? Perhaps it is because they find it difficult to celebrate who they really are, partly because of the pressure put on them to be someone else.

But then, celebrity and celebration are at very different ends of the spectrum of life. We are called to celebrate who we are and to rediscover relationships with people who will celebrate with us and with whom we can live in mutual dignity and respect. That has an important bearing on friendship. If we respect our friends, we will want the very best for them in all areas of life. But this means that friendship with someone who encourages us to follow certain lifestyle patterns such as binge drinking, taking drugs or sleeping around has to be questioned.

> **Friendship... is not something you learn in school. But if you haven't learned the meaning of friendship, you really haven't learned anything.**
> *Muhammad Ali*

Whether it is in our quality of friendship or in our view of ourselves, we often set low standards and suffer from these, settling for less than the best. Perhaps we succumb to the banal messages pumped out by our consumer society about how to acquire and then retain friends, how to be the real us by changing our look or more like the celebrities of our day by buying cheap high street imitations of the clothes they wear. And yet it can be so exhausting. Instead, we need to adopt the radical belief that life would be more enjoyable if we celebrated who we are as we are now, through acquiring the knowledge that we are loved regardless and are made to be us and no one else.

I don't think that it matters what we look like or what our experience of life is nor whether we are educated or whether we live in a big house.

If we are made by God, in the image of God, then we can celebrate our life.

3 'Don't feed the dark side, Luke'

Having celebrated what it means to be human, we need to come to terms now with a darker side of humanity. One of the many carrots placed in front of us, to keep us wanting more, is the idea of happiness. We are told that happiness is ours by right and being unhappy means that there is something fundamentally wrong with life.

And yet, deep down, we already know that there is a lot wrong with life, and maybe also with us. If we are to live as whole people, then we have to become experienced in handling both good and bad situations and dealing with right and wrong, because we can be sure that they will come our way at some point and, for most of us, on a daily basis.

'Growing up' is not simply about a matter of time passing or of getting taller; maturity is not about the onset of wrinkles. Instead, I would argue, both are about learning to live life to the full in a world that is deeply compromised but without sacrificing personal integrity. It means learning to move from the shallow end of life to deeper and riskier waters.

> **You're only young once, but you can be immature forever.**
> *Germaine Greer*

If we can take our eyes off ourselves for a minute, we might be able to see that life can be 'other-person centred'. This doesn't mean only living for somebody else when we are in love with them but applies to a wide variety of relationships. In other words, we try to see that what is happening in the lives of other people is at least as important – if not more so – than what is happening in our own.

Given the social assumptions that we are brought up with today, this is revolutionary thinking – the generator of a new kind of love which is not measured by how we feel but by the impact of our love on the other person.

It starts, of course, with those closest to us – our family and friends. But it also extends to school, college, work and the wider world, becoming a new way of living our life. It's as if we have been given a new pair of eyes and suddenly can see everything differently. This is the kind of love that required a new word to be used when it was described in the Bible.

Greek words already existed for friendship (*phileo*), erotic love (*eros*) and family love (*storge*) but this kind of love required something else. The word that was chosen, *agape*, described an unconditional, self-sacrificing love. It is a word that has been used since to describe people who have behaved sacrificially on behalf of others, whether in some small gesture of generosity or in martyrdom.

A distorted picture

We are all capable of such acts in our best moments and many of us would like to think that love is one of our main strengths but we are fighting against the tide of our own culture. Successive generations have been labelled 'the me generation', which is ironic since presumably only one generation can own that name. What is meant by this is not that we are all incredibly selfish, because we know that we are capable of acts of enormous generosity. The response to recent natural disasters such as the Asian Tsunami, the earthquakes in Pakistan and India and the Make Poverty History campaign shows that we can be generous in giving money and passionate about global justice.

No, what is meant is that we can still tolerate a culture growing up around us that panders to our every whim and which is not healthy, morally, spiritually or emotionally.

Rather than calling us 'the me generation' perhaps we should use the label 'the Jerry Springer generation', fascinated as we are by the small details of other people's lives, especially those who display their weaknesses on camera. We have become the generation of reality TV, epitomised by the phenomenon of *Big Brother*, the most famous reality TV show ever made. Running in thirty-one countries, over 100 series worldwide have been made since 2000.

But whether we are gripped or not by such programming, at the end of the day this is simply a cynical form of exploitative entertainment, part of the narcissistic society that surrounds us today. Just as Narcissus in the Greek myth looked at his own reflection in a pool of water so closely that he fell in and drowned, so we have become equally self-obsessed.

If we are a self-portrait of God, we should be able to look at ourselves in the mirror and see God in us. Our society, however, does everything to prevent this happening, giving us a distorted picture of ourselves and ensuring that we never know who we truly are.

Self-absorption

> **To knock over an idol, you must
> first get off your knees.**
> *R.H. Tawney*

At the beginning of the twenty-first century, this apparent obsession is not the reflection of a strong, rebellious ego. I don't think that many of us are shaking our fist at God and trying to create our own empire to rival religious faith. Quite the opposite. When we gaze at our reflection, we are looking for something or somebody, unsure of who we are. One of the reasons for this is that we have lost many of the reference points by which we used to judge behaviour, truth and beauty within our society.

Richard Sennett, writing in his book *The Fall of Public Man*, described narcissism as self-absorption, calling it an obsession with 'what this person, this event, means to me'. But the problem here is that because we are nearly always focused on self-gratification, we are denied fulfilment. We are always looking for something more, wanting our relationships to become 'more meaningful'. But in doing so, we are in the presence, once again, of longing and because we are investing it in ourselves and our own desires, we are unlikely to find fulfilment.

Just as in the previous chapter we saw how longing is invested in consumer society, here we see longing invested within our own emotional life. Sociologist David Lyon, writing in his book *The Steeple's Shadow*, described idolatry as being 'the investing of trust and hope in that which is unworthy of them and incapable of rewarding them'.

What we often end up doing is giving power to the wrong things within our lives. If as a generation we lack self-esteem and are constantly searching for the very thing that is going to fulfil us, then we might be tempted – like those floating in the water after a shipwreck – to grab anything around us to hang on to. What we don't realise, it seems, is that these things that we invest in and in which we place our trust begin to gain power over us. When this happens to an entire generation, as we see at present, then it becomes vulnerable and what started out as an act of freedom, branching out in a different direction from the previous generation, can end up as oppression.

> **I find it interesting that the meanest life, the poorest existence, is attributed to God's will, but as human beings become more affluent, as their living standard and style begin to ascend the material scale, God descends the scale of responsibility at commensurate speed.**
> *Maya Angelou*

Reversing good and evil

In the Bible there is a letter written by Paul, one of the main church leaders, to the church in Rome. In it he described a society that had become decadent and was falling apart. What characterised this society, he said, was that they had got to a stage where they called evil good and good evil. The people not only did things which were wrong, but they approved of others who did wrong. He was writing, of course, about Rome.

It was no surprise that Rome fell and never again became the power that it once had been. History shows that no society can continue to exist unless at its heart is a community that is committed to doing good and which regards wrongdoing and evil as something that should be judged and ultimately eradicated.

When we think of 'the law', we might think of the police, customs or government but the whole existence of the law presumes two things: first that we are good enough to keep it and secondly that we are bad enough to need it. Good law preserves this balance, granting us the freedom to express the good inside us but, when we do wrong, protecting the rest of society from us. That is why bad law is such a disaster. If obeying the law means you end up doing something wrong, then society begins to disintegrate.

> **I am the light of the world.**
> **Whoever follows me will never**
> **walk in darkness, but will have the**
> **light of life.**
> *Jesus*

By now, I hope, we should be aware of the need to celebrate life and the goodness within it but also the need to be aware of evil and to fight against it. Wanting a quiet life in a compromised world is the same as being compromised ourselves.

Being part of the problem

The problem is that we have got to start with ourselves. When we look at the big picture, we can see evil very clearly and are able to create a very long list of things that are definitely on the darker side of life. Issues such as organised crime, drug trafficking, prostitution, modern slavery, pornography and fraud we regard naturally as morally wrong.

However, things start to get more difficult when we look at ourselves because of the natural temptation to make excuses for our own behaviour. We may do something which is wrong but blame it on the circumstances or on our family upbringing. But, at some point, we have to admit that when the excuses run out, there may still be something that we need to admit to which comes under the column of wrongdoing or evil. This stark admission can be difficult to take. After all, most of us were brought up to be 'nice'. But if we look at our thought life or our actions, we find that we may have let ourselves down more than once between breakfast and lunch.

This is true of every human being who has ever lived or will ever live, with the exception of Jesus. We are all capable of doing wrong. It runs through us like lettering through a stick of rock. It spoils our character, brings hurt into our relationships and alienates families from one another. We can get up in the morning with the highest ideals and purest intentions, only to find that within a few minutes – or at least by the end of the day – we have succumbed to jealousy, anger, greed, lust or another ugly aspect of our character that we would rather deny even exists. We may have an affair and convince ourselves that it is OK because we 'really' love this person. But in doing so we will probably become quickly involved in telling lies, breaking someone's trust, breaking promises, being deceitful and hurting somebody we are meant to love. When we get involved in wrongdoing, it seems to breed other things that pull both us and others downwards. Often we realise that we are going downhill, however, and that we need to have someone to help us resist doing wrong and instead do what is good and right.

This does not mean that we are 100 per cent evil. Even Darth Vader, the 'baddy' in *Star Wars* had his good moments. We mustn't stop celebrating the goodness in either ourselves or the world. But it means that we must be realistic. If we are to retain any kind of integrity, we must recognise the fact that we are capable of doing many things that are bad and that some of us are capable of inflicting great pain on others. The question is what we do about it. It is easy to do wrong. It is doing good that is more difficult. But if we want to be at peace, to feel good about ourselves and to celebrate being alive, then we need to focus in on the good in life. History has shown that human beings can be reduced or even destroyed by succumbing to evil, either by passively accepting it or by actively doing it.

> **Non-cooperation with evil is a sacred duty.**
> *Mahatma Gandhi*

The problem is that Hollywood seems to focus in on acts of evil and newspapers run stories about bad things happening because in doing so, they sell more. And as a society, we are more interested in people having affairs and general scandal than in people having happy marriages and living lives of integrity. In fantasy then, it seems, evil can make the pulse race quicker, but in the long run evil promises much but delivers little, except perhaps increasing our addiction to it. Evils such as pornography, for instance, can be seductive and promise us instant pleasure. We feel anticipation and excitement but are left, at the end of the day, feeling shameful, guilty and anxious.

Is happiness the same as joy?

There does exist, however, a very old-fashioned word, which is joy. This is unlike happiness in that it can only be achieved if evil is overcome. Whereas happiness can coexist with delusion, joy cannot. People who retain a sense of joy may not be big thinkers or able to explain this quality in their lives but they will usually be people who at one time or another have come face to face with a darker side, whether it be suffering, evil, illness or bereavement.

> **For happiness one needs security, but joy can spring like a flower even from the cliffs of despair.**
> *Ann Morrow Lindbergh*

Joy is the light into which you enter at the end of a dark tunnel. It is based on having the courage to believe that none of us need be overwhelmed by our weaknesses, temptations or vulnerabilities or what happens to us in life. It admits to them but will not be conquered by them.

But many of us go through our entire lives without meeting anyone whose life is characterised by this sense of joy. We are satisfied with the calculus of happiness, trying to accumulate more things that make us happy than those things that make us sad. And yet one of the greatest enigmas for most of us who are material beings, desperately trying to 'keep happy', is that it is possible for those less fortunate than ourselves materially, or those suffering in other ways, to be joyful.

We watch TV documentaries about people who have very little compared to ourselves and see their faces etched with joy even though they have few prospects materially. This does not take away the fact that they could do with more material resources in their lives, but joy seems to be there in them anyway. And it leaves us asking, once each of us has 'enough' materially, are we experiencing joy in our lives?

The idea that happiness can be found through having more positive than negative things in our lives can also apply to the way that we approach goodness. Have we done more good things in life than bad? For some people, doing good works is their insurance policy, ensuring that if such a thing exists, their destiny after death is safe. As long as we do our best, then we can claim to have lived life to the full. But both the existence of God and the nature of God unfortunately upsets this neat theory. The issue is not only, I believe, that we have to be good in comparison with one another. We also have to ask whether we are concerned about meeting God's own standards and whether it is possible to have a relationship with God.

> **Jesus tapped me on the shoulder and said, 'Bob, why are you resisting me?' I said, 'I'm not resisting you!' He said, 'You gonna follow me?' I said, 'I've never thought about that before!' He said, 'When you're not following me, you're resisting me.'**
> *Bob Dylan*

But surely God's standards are impossibly high, much higher certainly than our personal assessment of the good works that we do?

Living in the light

We can view our own lives by comparing them to the life of Jesus Christ. If, as I believe, Jesus came down to earth to show us what it means to be a complete human being and to show us how we should be living, then it's likely that we will find ourselves both attracted and repulsed by this concept at the same time.

The good in us probably wishes that we could be more like that but then looks at some of the things Jesus both said and did and finds it impossible to imagine that we could ever follow in his footsteps. The bad in us is also likely to be repulsed by the scrutiny of Jesus' insight into what has gone wrong in our lives and, like Gollum in *The Lord of the Rings*, will probably look for some dark shadow to disappear into. Nevertheless, once God has been introduced into the picture, the question many of us end up asking is, 'how can these two things be reconciled?'

Someone once said that we are 'not as good as we should be' but not 'as bad as we could be'. This tension, between the good and bad in all of us, is a theme that is woven through human history.

> **If once you start down the dark path, forever it will dominate your destiny.**
> *Yoda to Luke in* Star Wars

Attempts to form utopian societies have always foundered because of our dark side. But equally, attempts to repress and oppress us have foundered on the love and goodness that each human being is capable of. Even in the concentration camps and gulags of the twentieth century, people helped one another and committed great acts of bravery on each other's behalf. Nevertheless, if we are to have a relationship with God, then we must be concerned with all evidence of wrongdoing within our lives and ask how it is that we can meet such impossibly high standards as we see through the life of Jesus and hear about through his teaching. As we shall see later on, however, it is God who has already provided the answer to this vital question.

For now, we'll focus in on some of the great issues of the day, and ask how we can wisely navigate our way through the many minefields in each of these areas.

4 Does size really matter?

So just how important is sex? Is the amount of time we spend thinking about it, doing it, watching it on TV and being targeted by advertising that uses its lure to get at us really warranted? Would we be less fulfilled as people if sex did not dominate our society to the extent that it does? In many ways, the West seems to be so addicted to sex that it regards its treatment of it as normal, natural and neutral. But in other parts of the world, a different attitude exists. In many countries, there is more restraint, a greater emphasis on the family and less overt use of sexual imagery to sell products. Of course to many people within the West, such societies are seen as repressive and our own as liberated. But what if it is the other way round? How did all this happen? How did we get here?

In the West in the early 1960s, boys still had hushed conversations about 'how far you could go'. Could you 'go horizontal', for instance? As sexual values changed, such conversations were seen to be the preserve of very conservative people, often with religious convictions. It became more and more acceptable to claim that you were enjoying an active sex life. But for most boys born in the 1950s and '60s, it seems that hormones ruled OK, masturbation was considered essential, if a little inadequate, and the vague hope that they might find a girl who would go further than was thought appropriate was the stuff of male fantasy. In truth, the possibility of finding a girl who would actually take her clothes off terrified most boys.

This was the time when much of the available pornography had the most confusing bits of a girl's anatomy airbrushed out. This ensured that women had a cloud hovering somewhere near the top of their thighs! *Playboy* magazine was around, *Penthouse* magazine was shortly to launch and the world was about to change dramatically, but things were, on the surface, still pretty much under control. I believe that change had to come because the ignorance of all things sexual was appalling. But the way in which it happened seems, with hindsight, to have been oppressive rather than liberating and began the rapid commercialisation of sex and spread of STDs (sexually transmitted diseases) which we have tried, and failed, to cope with ever since.

Doing your own thing

One of the things that happened in the 1960s was that young adults moved from adopting their parents' behaviour and beliefs to wanting to be radically different from them. This initially took the form of a protest against authority figures and institutions including parental authority, but also included the equal rights movement spreading rapidly across the United States, and its government's involvement in Vietnam.

It also included sex. The women's revolution sought equality for women as well as access to the pill to control their own fertility and sexual activity. It also called for increased access to nursery care for children so that women could go out to work. At the time, few imagined that as women grew in confidence both in the workplace and sexual relationships, this would have such a profound impact both on relationships between men and women and on male views of their own masculinity. It seemed that there were some men who no longer wanted to be committed to women if they could not have power over them.

Similarly it seemed that some women, wanting to be able to control when they had children because of work commitments, either chose not to have them or chose to have them without any biological father being involved as a committed parent. The glue, which in previous generations had kept men and women together, was quickly becoming unstuck.

But perhaps today the 1960s are best known for the extraordinary growth in freedom of sexual expression. Hippies waved placards on which were written the words, 'make love not war'. If you could get hold of it, there was rumoured to be something called 'free love' around. Marriage, previously the only traditional place for sexual intercourse, was brought into question and people began to live together without getting married.

> **When a marriage culture fails,**
> **sexual desire no longer unites;**
> **instead it fragments.**
> *Maggie Gallagher*

A recent survey conducted by the University of Sheffield found that, at least for women, sex outside an emotional relationship is an arid affair. In-depth interviews were conducted with forty-six women aged twenty-three to eighty-three. Nine out of ten said that they thought one night stands were immoral. They did not condemn those who did have them but said that there was 'something lacking in their lives'. They placed sex firmly in the context of an intimate relationship, admitting that when they had had 'casual sex' themselves, they were usually out of control in some way – on drink, drugs or just 'wanting love'.

Dr Sharron Hinchcliffe, one of the researchers on the project, said, 'sex is an emotional experience for women, so how could they have it without being emotionally involved?' This has to be set against the background of a society, described in the National Survey of Sexual Attitudes and Lifestyle (2001), which shows that women and men have more sexual partners than they had a decade before; are more likely to be unfaithful to them; are more likely to have paid for sex and more likely to have a sexually transmitted disease, most commonly Chlamydia. In her comments on the Sheffield report, Dr Sharron Hinchcliffe said that the survey had made her question whether women had really gained the sexual freedom they are supposed to have enjoyed since the 1960s.

But what if the problem is not with the women in the survey or even with women as a whole – since many more are having multiple partners – but with the very idea of sexual freedom? What if we were made for something very different?

Marriage: oppression or liberation?

What Christianity has to say about sex can often be a surprise to a lot of people. Christians are often stereotyped as being essentially negative about sex. If that is true then it is a shame, because that is not the Bible's attitude. In fact, one book of the Bible is devoted entirely to a celebration of sex and intimacy! However, the church has often seemed to rank sexual wrongdoing as more important than greed, pride or even religious hypocrisy.

In this book, I quote 'agony aunt' Deirdre Sanders, who says that something has gone horribly wrong with young people and sex. Perhaps it is that the sex we are being sold in our culture is inadequate and unfulfilling. Until quite recently, sex was commonly seen as a private celebration of love between two people following the making of strong and binding promises before family and friends. In making a public declaration that a relationship was exclusive, the couple had decided to make a public declaration that it was both permanent and procreative. It wasn't hidden or private, fragile or temporary, or a relationship where pregnancy would be seen as an awkward complication or where the paternity of the child would be uncertain.

> **Marriage is a wonderful invention: then again, so is a bicycle repair kit.**
> *Billy Connolly*

Sex was the seal on this agreement but came after this public declaration, not before. It was a seal on the relationship, an indication that it had reached the stage where these things could now become a reality. And many people waited to have sex because they wanted to know that they were both ready to make a commitment and such a statement. Within this context, sex is seen as enormously important but placed within obvious limits. Let loose, as it seemingly is today, it can destroy rather than affirm relationships.

But marriage is not just about the relationship itself. It is about something more. It is a third factor in the relationship, existing beyond the feelings of the couple at any one time. As novelist and poet Judith Viorst once said, if you fall out of love, marriage is there to keep you together until you fall in love again.

> **For a marriage relationship to flourish, there must be intimacy. It takes an enormous amount of courage to say to your spouse, 'This is me. I'm not proud of it – in fact, I'm a little embarrassed by it – but this is who I am.'**
> *Bill Hybels*

It is also a time when two families become related to one another. In our individualistic society, we often think of relationships as private and individual but in many societies, a large part of the public celebration is the coming together of two families. Marriage, through its commitment to permanence, allows two families the opportunity to come together, even though the couple getting married needs to be given space to form a new family unit themselves.

> **After about 20 years of marriage, I'm finally starting to scratch the surface of that one [*what women want*]. And I think the answer lies somewhere between conversation and chocolate.**
> *Mel Gibson*

Staying together

I often ask couples who have been living together for some time whether their relationship has changed in any way since they have got married. Many of them say that they feel more secure. One couple I spoke to, however, had just moved in together rather than get married. She said that the difference between going out together and living together was that their relationship was now permanent, saying, 'we can't get rid of one another now.' His response was, 'yes we can. Of course we can.' An awkward silence ensued. Although they were very much in love, there was nothing to stop the key being left on the mantelpiece or the wardrobe being emptied of clothes. No public promises were made, no marriage licence was issued. It all depended on wanting to stay together. But what about when we don't want to stay together?

By now, however, some readers might want to point to the statistics of marriage breakdowns. And it does seem that marriages are breaking down all over the place with nearly one in two in the UK not lasting. So we might ask why marriage is any better than living together or even having sex with a number of boyfriends or girlfriends to increase, what pop therapy magazine *Psychologies* called, our 'sexual intelligence'.

But one of the ironies is that those who wish to cohabit, seeing marriage as oppressive, restrictive or just unnecessary, experience a higher rate of relationship breakdown than married couples. Statistics also show that couples who live together before they get married are more likely to separate than those who don't. After all, how can you have a trial relationship for something that is essentially meant to be permanent? They are different experiences. It seems that separating pleasure from responsibility detracts in some way from the significance of the relationship for us.

Of course some people still believe that living together is an inadequate expression of a permanent relationship. Yet few raise objections. Parents may want to complain, but if they wish to continue to have a relationship with their children, they have to keep quiet. And for many young people, moving in together is a step that is not taken lightly.

In other words, it is seen as an indication that the relationship has moved onto a new level. It may not be seen as the final stage, as the prospect of marriage could still be a possibility. Friends may congratulate the couple, a party may be held to celebrate. The idea then that this is 'living in sin' is often seen as old-fashioned. But the concept is also often completely misunderstood by couples. After all, they are just celebrating their love and making a deeper commitment. Aren't they?

> **Marriage has a unique place because it speaks of an absolute faithfulness, a covenant between radically different persons, male and female; and so it echoes the absolute covenant of God with his chosen, a covenant between radically different partners.**
> *Rowan Williams*

Yet marriage promises so much more than this. For a Christian, it is a deeply spiritual commitment. The promises made at a Christian wedding are promises made not only to a husband or wife before friends and family, but

also before God and to God. It is a joyful event but a
solemn, thoughtful joy. It commits itself to the future and not just to the present; to the worst to come and not just the best. This makes marriage joyful because it brings God right into the heart of it.

One young couple, married when they were both twenty-two and now twenty-five, told me of their own particular excitement and joy about marriage:

Chris: 'What I love about marriage is the feeling of being in an unbreakable team of two. It can sometimes feel as if the whole world is falling apart around us, but deep down we both know all will be well because whatever happens, we have one another. We believe in this and strive to ensure that we will always have each other's love, support, loyalty and commitment.

'I'm also deeply proud of my wife. Of course, we can bicker and be grumpy with each other but I know that she knows that I'm proud of her. I look across the room when we are out with friends and smile and think, "that's my wife!" – she's made the biggest commitment anyone could make to another person and she made it to me – I don't want to let her down.'

Bex: 'Being married means you can throw yourself fully into the relationship, being able to plan into the future, decorate the house, have children together, make mutual friends... and not be worrying when it might end.

'Marriage often sounds boring but it's not, it's fun, real fun, like the fun you can have with only your closest of friends or family – knowing you're truly loved. Being able to be yourself also means you can be free to share your dreams, try something new, make a fool of yourself, discuss how you really feel. And it's great seeing a side of your other half that you know no one else will ever see and revealing who you really are to that person alone.'

A high view of sex

So through marriage, Christianity celebrates sex. Indeed, it has a much higher view of sex than popular culture, even though magazines, soap operas and advertising seem to focus on little else. But it's because it has such a high view of sex and what sex signifies, and because it delights in sexual pleasure, that it wants to let society know that it is missing out. As Deirdre Sanders commented, a lot of people are not enjoying sex and feel that they have been short changed.

> **I think there's a whole generation, or generations of young people, who are not... having a good time, they're picking up infections which are going to damage them physically, some of them aren't going to know that they're not going to have children as a result of this, they're not having good sex, they're not enjoying this, they're not having relationships they're finding rewarding.**
>
> *Deirdre Sanders, agony aunt for* The Sun *newspaper*

But to understand why Christianity has such a high view of sex, we have to turn back to the beginning of the Bible, to the story of how humanity was made in the image of God. The story goes that when God first made a sole individual, this arrangement turned out to be inadequate as there was obviously no possibility of a relationship with another person. Then woman was made and it was together that the two people adequately expressed the image of God. They came from one flesh (Eve was formed out of Adam's ribs) and the Bible speaks of sexual intercourse being the rejoining of men and women back into that intimate union which is 'one flesh'.

That 'oneness' is the intimacy which we all long for but which, I believe, we can never achieve without commitment to one partner for life. Here again, we see 'longing' reappearing. It is destined to reappear whenever something has a deep spirituality. And certainly sex is intimately related to spirituality even though everything in Western society fights against this. Yet both are expressions of something that is embedded deep within us. If we are not committed, we will never discover this.

Yet cohabitation is not the opposite of marriage. Far from it. Both are expressions of people who love one another and want to be together even if one may fall short of the other. The opposite of intimacy is sex without relationship. It rejects the realism of the imperfect but glorious mess of human love for a delusional half-life expressed through fantasy. Perhaps this is why our culture has so many problems over sex. The kind of sex that we are sold today is not the intimate loving relationship sort, between two fallible people who will get it wrong sometimes, are not hugely good looking or only want to make love infrequently because that is what suits them. No. We are driven by fantasies that we cannot realise, describing people that we will never be, for whom sex is apparently the number one motivating drive and number one priority.

Whatever shape sex comes in today, it's an expression of the increasing pornographic imagination that is rapidly infiltrating our sexual thinking but which is essentially non-relational. Pornography prefers illusion to intimacy. It does not enhance relationships; it makes people feel inadequate by contrast. It does not create love; it destroys it. It does not liberate; it is addictive. It creates excitement but ends in shame. It is not spiritual; it is mechanical. It is not open; it is secretive. It presents itself as a beautiful woman, but in truth is a rotting corpse.

From a Christian standpoint, sex is different. It is not about illusion but about two vulnerable people being committed, with all that entails. It is not delusional in that both people have to be honest and transparent about who they are, which can be painful. And yet it is an intense expression of creativity and joy. It needs a sense of humour as it lurches from the sublime to the ridiculous. It involves passion yet requires understanding when one or both are tired and distracted. It is tender but physical. It welcomes the comfort of the hug as well as the excitement of the orgasm. It strives to keep a balance between the selfless and the selfish, between being in control and being out of control, between love and lust.

But regardless of whether any particular occasion leads to disappointment or ecstasy, it's a unique world created by two people in which no one else lives and in which they should not need to care about what anybody else does or thinks. As the Old Testament's Song of Solomon would have it, they make love in a 'high-walled garden'. This relationship thrives on a permanent commitment in which two people are able to relax and explore each other, 'till death us do part'.

The gay revolution

In terms of shifts in sexual attitudes, one of the most marked is in attitudes to homosexuality. Over the last fifty

years, homosexual men and women have moved from
being forced to remain silent about their sexual orientation
to being able to form 'civil partnerships' which are legally
recognised. Homosexual behaviour was unlawful (for men)
in the UK but in the 1960s, things began to change. In
1967, the Sexual Offences Act was passed that legalised
gay sex in private for anyone over the age of twenty-one.
This marked a sea change where it became increasingly
acceptable to be gay. Of course, not everything changed
overnight but with shifting sexual values in other areas of
society also, it was inevitable that gay people would see a
marked change in their status.

Why then can homosexuality still be such a painful
issue? There are few areas of sexual expression where
listening to one another is as important and yet it is so
little practised. Often the barriers that divide people are
made up of mistaken assumptions, false stereotypes and a
preference for dogmatism rather than love. Many people
are against homosexuality because they mistakenly
associate it with paedophilia and abuse for some bizarre
reason. Others stereotype gay people in ways that are
unhelpful and which have no basis in reality. But on the
surface, European society is becoming more tolerant of gay
relationships even if this is not so in many other parts of
the world. And yet Christians who believe that homosexual
practice is acceptable are still in the minority. Why is this?

One reason is the fact that Christianity takes a very high
view of marriage, as we have seen. Its vision of one man,
one woman for life as the norm for sexual commitment
may underwrite heterosexual relationships, but in doing so,
also undermines homosexual relationships. Its vision of sex
as procreative provides a *raison d'être* for heterosexual sex
which cannot be the case for homosexual sex. Christianity
also views same-sex intercourse as working against the

way the body was designed rather than with it, thereby ensuring that Christianity has not sanctioned homosexual behaviour.

Christians do not have the freedom to pluck any belief out of thin air and call it Christian. One of the reference points for the Christian faith is the belief in the authority of the Bible and that its interpretation is a matter for the church community as a whole rather than for any particular individual. Most Christians believe that the Bible does not sanction gay sex; while it speaks of it infrequently, it always does so critically. In fact, although many attitudes change over the thousands of years covered by the Bible such as the role of slaves or the position of women in society, the Bible does not seem to change its attitude to homosexual behaviour. It seems then that there is little room to manoeuvre unless we wish to reinterpret the text.

However, some Christians have done precisely this, arguing that what the Bible is really talking about in the few stories, commands, objections and lists of practices that include homosexuality, is gang rape, underage sex, temple prostitution and other practices which most people, both gay and straight, would object to. They argue that the Bible does not comment on the idea of long-term, monogamous, same-sex relationships between two people who love one another faithfully.

It is this idea of a loving, faithful, same-sex couple that presents most difficulties for those Christians who do not agree with gay sex. There seems to be so many positive things at work here. Besides companionship, there is mutual support and many other benefits that come from two people sharing their lives together. Surely these are things that we can all accept as being good? After all, if society has publicly acknowledged the presence of civil partnerships, why can't Christians? However, if a sexual component is present, the question still exists of whether it is acceptable within a Christian worldview. While the Bible does not appear to say anything negative about homosexual orientation or identity, it is strongly critical of homosexual behaviour.

So there are two issues at stake. One is the acceptability of gay sex; the other is the authority of the Bible in twenty-first century society. This means that the issue is painful for all concerned. A person, for example, who is gay but also a Christian is left with a dilemma. The only alternative to doing something which is considered wrong by the majority of Christians is to remain celibate without any possibility of settling down with somebody for life. But someone who is already living with their gay partner might be told that they cannot be a Christian since they are 'living in sin', even if they feel that the love they are experiencing from their partner is a blessing from God.

Yet it is also true that those who believe that homosexual practice is wrong can be vilified and stereotyped as homophobic when often this is not the case. There can also be pain felt here as homophobia is a particularly horrible form of discrimination and yet it is sometimes used, unfairly, to label all those who hold either conservative Christian or even secular beliefs on this issue. After all, the word is defined as 'an extreme and irrational aversion to homosexuals'. It is sad then that the word 'homophobia' is increasingly being used as an indiscriminate insult for anybody who disagrees with any aspect of gay culture.

But for many Christians, there is a tension between honouring the message of the Bible about the place of sex within marriage, and loving those around them from whatever background and orientation. It is a tension which may also be felt in relationships with gay friends but it is precisely because of this that everyone should offer others the love and generosity which they dare to hope may be offered to them.

Being single

Many people remain single despite wanting to be in a relationship and they feel that the prospects of meeting a suitable partner within the near future are remote. It never seems to happen. We may be offered fleeting sexual relationships but this is not what we want. And it can be deeply painful. Whether we are sixteen and everybody else in the class has boyfriends or girlfriends, or thirty with all our friends having found a partner, or even forty with 'the clock ticking', being single can feel like rejection. It can feel like sitting in the waiting room with everybody staring at us as if we have missed our train, or that we are playing in the second division, or even that there is something wrong with us that nobody will tell us about.

Of course friendship can be really important here, as we shall see. But it may not cover the desire that is deeply rooted in all of us – the desire to have somebody with whom we can share our lives in all respects. Few of us would consider our life as being fulfilled through permanent celibacy. What is important, however, is whatever the pressures on us and within us, that we retain our integrity, live for others and lovingly nurture the friendships that we have.

Being single and celibate in the long term can also be very difficult. There is no point in stating otherwise. People can suddenly become single through the death of their partner, separation or divorce and the grief and pain can add to the loneliness which a sudden loss of whatever sort might bring. It's at these times, however, that some people find that God becomes very real to them and that they discover a reality they never knew existed before – the unconditional love of God.

But being single in the long term does not mean that the energy one would normally put into a relationship has to be dissipated and lost. I have met many people across the world who are both positive and enthusiastic about life despite – or maybe even because of – being single, whether it is in the short or long term. These are often people who have committed themselves to serving others in some way. They can be found in all areas of the world working as volunteers, teachers, youth workers, nurses, doctors, engineers. They often have the time and energy to throw themselves into situations which those who are married do not have.

> **The human race has been set up. Someone, somewhere, is playing a practical joke on us. Apparently, women need to feel loved to have sex. Men need to have sex to feel loved. How do we ever get started?**
> Billy Connolly

It is perhaps the height of irony given our current culture that when the apostle Paul was writing about these things to the church in Corinth, he said that he wanted the Christians there to be as free as possible in order to pursue their calling. He realised that married people could do this but also knew that marriage brought what he called 'distractions'. As far as he was concerned being married and being single were both gifts but he wished that people could be like him, free to have more time to serve God.

That's directly opposite to the message that our society is currently giving!

I believe that the world needs more people like Paul. How many people have there been in the world who have acted as an inspiration to countless others but who could never have achieved what they did had they been married? Being married and being single are of course very different but being single is not an inferior option in any way and often can be an advantage.

The desire for friendship

The quote by Billy Connolly shows us that although we all want to experience fulfilment sexually, we also desire love, and yet they are not the same thing. We all crave intimacy with someone, whether it's with a sexual partner, a friend or within our family. Intimacy is difficult to describe but we find that longing is at the heart of it. There is a restlessness in all of us that is only satisfied when we find someone who loves us and who loves us for who we are now, yet, at the same time, challenges us to excellence in all that we are and all that we do.

> **It takes a great deal of courage to stand up to your enemies, but even more to stand up to your friends.**
> *J. K. Rowling*

Both the acceptance and the challenge are needed. Yet often we are not secure enough to accept the second part of this. We want to find someone, whether a soulmate or a friend, who will accept us for who we are, 'warts and all', but if that person challenges us, then we often accuse them of not accepting us and instead wanting to change us. But there is a significant difference between someone who has entered a competition in *Zoo* magazine to win breast implants for his girlfriend and somebody who is trying to help us change patterns of behaviour that may be damaging the person we really are.

I recently read a book where the author commented that the state of friendship was at its lowest ebb for hundreds of years. Friendships between men can be difficult because of the fear that they might be considered gay and friendships between men and women can be difficult because of living in an over-sexualised society that seemingly rules out platonic friendships. Instead of this, we have 'mates'. Yet mates are often kept at some kind of distance, not always experiencing the intimacy of true friendships. They might not share in the mutual vulnerability of being open enough to admit weaknesses and fears as well as strengths and successes.

> **I still find trusting people quite hard. I've got a couple of mates that I do let in, but that's it. It's something I've got to sort out – I cut people off.**
> *Robbie Williams*

Men, in particular, can find it difficult to move from having 'mates' to having friends. A sad story explains the difference. Three young men were drinking in a bar. They were mates. Two of them said that they were going to a café for food and the third said that he would join them but that he had to go home first. He never showed up at the café. The next day he was found dead in his bed having committed suicide. Why? He had just been 'dumped' by his girlfriend. Questioned about whether they knew anything, his two mates said, 'no, it's not the kind of thing you talk about with your mates.'

> **Friendship is born at that moment when one person says to another, 'what you too? I thought I was the only one.'**
> *C.S. Lewis*

We might argue that we do have friends in that sense who would share such stuff with us but many men, in particular, do not and the absence of friendship in our society is becoming a real problem. Rising divorce rates, increasingly long hours spent at work and a culture of individualism, as well as high mobility as people move about frequently, means that it is often difficult to form the long-term friendships that we long for.

Desiring the best

But there is another reason why the state of friendship is in crisis. In previous generations, one of the key components of friendship was that friends would desire *moral* excellence for us. They would encourage us morally and spiritually and we would do the same for them. When we succumbed to temptation, they would pick us up and help us.

In our own society today, however, who is committed to moral excellence? Do we even know what this is? When a friend rings up and invites us to go out on the town, where getting wasted is routine, can we honestly say that they have our best interests at heart? Might some of our friends not cause us to lose our self-respect and self-control?

Friendship and intimacy are born out of honesty and mutual respect. True friendship is about the mutual expression of love. The Greek word for it is *phileo*. It is a friendship love rather than an erotic love (*eros*). It was mirrored in the relationship that Jesus had with his followers as well as the self-sacrificial love they called *agape*. But to love is to be vulnerable; it is to be open with one another, realising that there is a dark side to our personality. That means that we inevitably take risks when we open up to one another.

How extraordinary it is that the Bible repeatedly claims that God loves us unconditionally while being able to see all that is in our hearts. If that is true, then God is love personified – and a true friend to whom we can open up without worry about what he will say. Yet God is also a friend who will call us to excellence in the way that we live our lives.

5 The meaning of life

Hearing that she is pregnant can often be either one of the most wonderful or one of the worst moments in a woman's life. One woman, Anna, had given up hope of ever having a child only to hear the fantastic news that she is going to have a baby. Sally, on the other hand, feels that her world has been turned upside down. She can't remember who she slept with at the party, her parents will be horrified when they hear and her education is probably going to be interrupted, putting on hold the dreams she had for the future. Both know that if everything goes well, in approximately nine months' time they will be having a baby – bringing a new life into the world. But hundreds of thousands of women like Sally, who react with shock to the news that they are pregnant, face the critical decision as to what to do. Do they keep the baby and become a mother, have the baby and give it up to be adopted, or have an abortion? One thing that we do know is that whatever Sally is thinking of doing, she will need all the information and support she can get to help her during what will be a very difficult period in her life.

Before the 1967 Abortion Act was passed by the UK parliament, there were up to 20,000 abortions carried out legally. After the Act was passed, the number escalated so greatly that in 2004, 185,400 abortions were carried out in the UK that year. In the US, following the liberalising of abortion in the *Roe vs Wade* case ruled on by the Supreme Court in 1973, 1.3 million abortions were carried out in 2005.

The 1967 UK Act was meant to make it safer and less problematic for a woman who needed an abortion to obtain one. Before this period many women went to 'back street' abortionists whose facilities were inadequate and who were often incompetent. As a result, women's health suffered and some even died.

The law in the UK today is that before a foetus has reached the age of twenty-four weeks, two doctors must decide that the risk to a woman's physical or mental health or the risk to her child's physical or mental health will be greater if she continues with the pregnancy than if she ends it. However, because of what happened before 1967, there is no time limit on abortion where two doctors agree that a woman's health or life is gravely threatened by continuing with the pregnancy or that the foetus is likely to be born with severe physical or mental abnormalities.

Perspectives on pregnancy

How are Anna and Sally likely to think about the significance of their pregnancy? Anna in welcoming her pregnancy is likely to be thinking of it as a human life from the earliest moments. As one writer has commented, she will view her pregnancy as an offer of hospitality. This after all is what her womb was designed for and a new human life is growing within it. Yet even where the baby is wanted and eagerly awaited, the growing sophistication in technology for screening for abnormalities within the womb ensures that those who are eagerly expecting a baby are going to have to face more and more complex and painful choices.

However, Sally, who is considering an abortion, may be more ambivalent. She will find it difficult to view what is going on in her womb in quite the same way as Anna, who is celebrating. What are her other options?

First, she may choose to minimise the status of the embryo (which later becomes known as a foetus). The embryo could be thought of as a 'thing' – an object rather than a human subject. After all, it is invisible, there is no movement which can be felt and in its earliest days it is little more than a collection of cells. This 'thing' could be thought of as the possession of the prospective mother. It is Sally's body after all and she has the right to do with it as she wishes. She has the right to choose and since, in her view, the embryo is not a person then there are few if any moral implications. But even here Sally may feel a sense of loss. There is no avoiding the fact that if everything had gone well, a baby would have been born. She is still faced with 'what might have been', even if in having the abortion she feels that she made the right decision given the circumstances. She also needs to know that there are still health risks both physically and emotionally in having an abortion.

Secondly, the presence of the embryo might be thought of as an invasion of Sally's life in a more general sense, especially as the circumstances in which she became pregnant were unfortunate and the pregnancy was unplanned. It is certainly a 'disruption' of a woman's life and constitutes a basis for 'emergency' contraception (commonly known as the morning-after pill) should the woman immediately suspect that she is pregnant after unprotected intercourse. Abortion is seen here as solving a problem. It is a response to the difficulties in which Sally finds herself, even if it is regrettable. These reasons are to do with Sally's life. With this view, of course, Sally's life takes precedence and the embryo receives little, if any, consideration. But as the pregnancy proceeds, and more is known about what is happening in the womb, it becomes more difficult to avoid treating the foetus as a human being or believe that the only life that matters is one's own.

> **I have met thousands and thousands of pro-choice men and women. I have never met anyone who is pro-abortion. Being pro-choice is not being pro-abortion. Being pro-choice is trusting the individual to make the right decision for herself and her family, and not entrusting that decision to anyone wearing the authority of government in any regard.**
> *Hilary Clinton*

According to research done by the The Alan Guttmacher Institute in New York, half of all pregnancies to American women are unplanned. Half of these end in abortion and at current rates about one in three American women will have had an abortion by the time she reaches the age of forty-five. In the US, a survey conducted in 1987 that polled 1,900 women, found that the most common reasons for having an abortion were that the baby would interfere with school, work or other responsibilities and that they could not afford a child.

In 2004, a survey was completed by 1,209 abortion patients at eleven large medical centres for the The Alan Guttmacher Institute. In depth interviews were conducted with thirty-eight women. The reasons most frequently quoted were that having a baby would disrupt a woman's work, education or ability to care for the child (74 per cent); that she could not afford a baby at this time (73 per cent) or that she did not want to be a single mother or was having relationship problems (48 per cent). Nearly four out of ten women said that they had finished their childbearing, and almost one-third were not yet ready to have a child. Less than 1 per cent said that their parents' or partners' wish for them to have an abortion was the most important reason. Younger women also often reported that they were unprepared for the transition to being mothers, while older women regularly cited their responsibility to existing dependants.

But in the conclusions to their survey, the authors said:

> In light of the public debate over the morality of abortion, it is notable that the women in our survey emphasized their conscious examination of the moral aspects of their decisions. Although some described abortion as sinful and wrong, many of those same women, and others, described the indiscriminate bearing of children as a sin, and their abortion as 'the right thing' and 'a responsible choice'. Respondents also often acknowledged the complexity of the decision, and described an intense and difficult process of deciding to have an abortion, which took into account the moral weight of their responsibilities to their families, themselves and children they might have in the future.

So these women at least reflected upon the morality of their decision. Yet the wide variety of reasons given ensures that we cannot use a mother's attitude (or both parents if a father is involved in the decision) to her pregnancy to determine whether or not the embryo is a human being and what the consequences of that would be on having an abortion. It is here that the battleground for the ethical debate on abortion lies, focusing in on the issue of 'when does a human being exist?' or 'what does it means to be a person?'

What is a person?

This may at first seem a little obscure. But somewhere in the transition from an embryo to a baby, there has to be a point at which deliberately getting rid of the baby could be seen arguably as infanticide and, therefore, tantamount to murder. The question is therefore whether such a line can be drawn, where it should be drawn and what the impact is of that decision on judging whether abortion is morally right or wrong. Three positions exist which are worth considering.

First, there is the position that argues that abortion is always wrong. This is because it fails to respect the right to life of the foetus. Such a position leads to the belief that life begins when sperm and egg come together to form the fertilised egg. So the moment of conception is when human life begins. Many people also worry that a foetus being aborted because of an impairment is a negative comment on those with disabilities within our society. Who is to decide whether the quality of life of a foetus will be so low that it should be aborted? A friend of mine was once speaking at a conference where one speaker said she thought that it would be best if foetuses with a certain disability were aborted. One of the speakers following her was a person with that exact disability. How did they both feel?

But even with such a viewpoint, people who are totally

opposed to abortion and are labelled 'pro life', might allow it under certain circumstances such as rape, child abuse or incest. In such cases, the pregnancy could be seen as prolonging the assault itself. It's also worth mentioning that, to be consistent, people who hold such a view should also be opposed to those forms of contraception which prevent the fertilised egg from implanting in the womb such as IUDs or the morning-after pill.

The second position is taken by those who are in favour of the wide availability of abortion facilities and who are often referred to as 'pro-choice'. I've already written that the emphasis is on the woman's right to choose what happens to her own body. In such a situation, the foetus is thought to have either no rights or very few and what rights it does have are outweighed by those of a person already born. However, the quotation from Hilary Clinton shows that to be pro-choice does not necessarily mean to be pro-abortion. It means that, after all is said and done, the person who has to make the final decision is a woman, with her partner if he is involved, and with those others such as family, medical practitioners, employers and friends who have some part to play in the decision and its subsequent consequences.

> **Abortion is advocated only by persons who have themselves been born.**
> *Ronald Reagan*

The third position is the middle ground which argues that abortion is allowable under certain circumstances. The middle ground here steers between the absolute right to life of the foetus and the absolute right to choose of the woman; between total prohibition and abortion on demand. This is based on the idea that the foetus is potentially human and acquires status and rights as it grows. For this reason, this view encourages abortions to take place earlier rather than later. In the UK in 2004, 88 per cent of abortions were in fact carried out at under thirteen weeks' gestation and 60 per cent were under ten weeks' gestation. Similar statistics apply in the US also.

One of the key factors to consider here is implantation, which occurs at the beginning of the second week. Some would say that before this point, the fertilised egg is fragile and could be washed out of the woman's body by the next menstrual flow. However, on implantation in the side of the womb, the true relationship with the mother begins.

After these two points, conception and implantation, it becomes more difficult to pick any particular stage at which one can say 'it is at this point that human life begins.' Could it be when the foetus feels pain or when its brain begins to develop or even when it can survive outside the womb? There are arguments for and against each stage. Viability is, after all, possible earlier and earlier so that the survival of pre-term babies at twenty-three or twenty-four weeks is now almost routine.

What do Christians have to say about all of this? Of course, they take up different positions but most Christians seem to be pro-life. This does not mean that they do not respect the difficult choices that women have to make but they want to defend the right to life of the foetus because they believe that his or her life is God given and it is not for us to take it away. Psalm 139, for instance, talks about God making us in our mother's womb. The prophet Jeremiah quotes God as having said to him, 'before I formed you in the womb I knew you'. This introduces a new language. Rather than the language of rights, this speaks of the love of God through creating us as unique human beings. Here we come full circle to the awe-inspiring vision of who we are in the opening chapter. In other words, we are a person because God has made us a person. This does not mean that there are not difficult decisions to make but it provides us with a definition of what it means to be a person. This is based on relationships. First with God and then with others, including prospective parents, friends and wider family. The emphasis is always 'choose life'. Even if the baby is adopted – choose life.

Watch me grow

As I've already said, one of the problems is that in the past the foetus has been invisible. It was therefore difficult to relate to it as 'him' or 'her'. More recently, however, ultrasound technology has enabled prospective parents to see the foetus moving in the womb and maybe even to take home a picture (albeit a hazy one). And recently, things have also changed with regards to our relationship with what is going on in the womb.

The work of Professor Stuart Campbell of London's Create Health Clinic has brought about a new kind of ultrasound that can produce 4D video images of the foetus in the womb with a startling clarity. Twelve-week-old foetuses can be seen 'walking' in the womb. They appear, at a later stage, to yawn, rub their eyes and even smile. But this new technology has unnerved and angered some pro-choice professionals, who see this as bringing undue pressure to bear on people when they are most vulnerable. And yet perhaps the opposite is true. Such pictures show more accurately the nature of our decision. They make it more difficult to see 'it' as anything other than a person, especially when we can enjoy pictures of a foetus appearing to smile in the womb. These human characteristics are unnerving when some of them take place under twenty-four weeks, the limit up to which abortion is allowed. This is why it's arguable that the foetus has to be taken into account in any decision, as it is no longer as invisible or as inanimate as it once was.

It is interesting that in the UK recently, there has been a large increase in the number of Members of Parliament who wish to reduce the time limit during which an abortion can take place. The new pictures which have become available have been one of the reasons for this change, as has the availability of new technology leading to viability below the abortion limit. This is the shock of recognition – something has become someone.

Recognition and respect

Having a relationship with another human being has, at the heart of it, two elements. The first is recognition and the second is respect. Recognition comes in two forms: a statement and an invitation. A statement that somebody else is a human being, causing us to respond to them by giving them the dignity and freedoms which are the due of every human being. They are not a thing, they are not even an animal; they are a 'person'.

Secondly, recognition is an invitation to see humanity in a person whom others may choose to ignore or treat with indifference. Powerless people without a voice have always been overlooked and had their wishes disregarded and, as a result, someone has always had to champion their cause if it is to be heard. It is easy to say that someone similar to ourselves is a human being and to give them our time and attention, making them a priority in our lives, but we need to go further than that. We need to realise that everyone should be treated as human beings and recognise that they are as human as we are. Recognition of humanity is the beginning of relationship.

The second element is respect. Not only do we need to recognise somebody as a human being but we need to respect them as a unique person. All human beings share something in common: we are the same underneath. But it is equally true that we are essentially different. Recognition is therefore about recognising 'the sameness' in each of us and respect is about respecting the 'difference' between us. Respecting another human being, however, takes care and attention to detail. There is a story to be told, a context to be understood. We need to consider the life the other person is living and the things which are important for them. Not to listen is to displace their story with our assumptions. Recognition and respect are at the heart of relationship and listening is important to that relationship because listening conveys love.

This recognition and respect should be at the heart of three different sets of relationships. First, it should be at the heart of the wider debate on abortion. Unfortunately it is not. Stereotyping, entrenched positions, bigotry, prejudice and even physical violence have scarred this debate, sometimes even perpetrated by people who claim to have God on their side.

Secondly, recognition and respect need to be present when we are with someone who is distressed and unsure of themselves and is trying to find their way forward. This is a time to listen to their story rather than condemn or dogmatically preach at them.

Thirdly, recognition and respect need to be offered also to the foetus by all involved in making the decision about his or her future. In other words the burden of proof should lie with those who do not think the foetus should be considered a human being. If this does not happen, then the foetus will be ignored in the rush to make suitable arrangements. It is too important a decision to leave this stage out just because the strident, dogmatic and often unsympathetic nature of those who are 'pro-life' puts others off.

The foetus cannot speak, yet we need to 'listen' to him or her and ask whether it is appropriate to offer that recognition of our shared humanity and respect for a person's uniqueness. Only after having been willing to consider that he or she is a person with whom we are having a relationship can we consider the way forward, whatever the final decision is. To refuse to do that is to assume that the foetus is an object rather than a human being, property rather than humanity. Such a willingness to include the foetus in the relationships we are building, even as we make our decision, is only fair.

Convenience, efficiency and comfort

Perhaps the problem facing us, and one that lies at the heart of this whole debate, is confusion about our own humanity. If we don't have a high opinion of our own humanity, regarding ourselves as here by chance, and if we have tacitly taken on board the idea that personally, we are a tradable commodity within a disposable society, then it should be no surprise that the sum of the values that we apply to ourselves, we apply to the foetus.

Some of the highest values within our society are those of convenience, efficiency and comfort. They are highly prized and dominate many of our lifestyle choices but they can also be seen as lying behind some of the reasons as to why women might have an abortion, as painful as that decision is. If abortion is a life or death decision, can it also be a lifestyle choice?

The issue is not whether we have particular religious or spiritual beliefs on which we base our attitude to abortion but instead, as we have seen above, whether we believe that the foetus is a human from the point of conception or even at implantation. If we do believe this, then perhaps this should take equal priority with the issue of what the impact of the pregnancy will be personally and socially.

These are delicate and painful issues, and if we were to consider all the factors that go into how we should treat the foetus, we would find that we had a very long list of questions. The main one, however, is whether we are terminating the life of a human being or just a thing. After all, we know that by doing nothing but letting time pass, we will be giving birth to a human being in just nine months' time. Even in the tangled web of emotions and morals in the American series *Sex in the City*, when Charlotte wants to have a child but can't, the value of a pregnancy becomes something important. This forces all of those involved to look again at their own decisions, including abortions that they have had in the past or may intend to have in the future.

> **Too many people use abortion as a form of birth control. And that's very wrong. I could never, ever have an abortion.**
> *Brooke Shields*

What if Sally decides, after looking at the option of being a mother or of having the baby adopted, that she is going to have an abortion anyway? Those who do not think that abortion is the right way forward will find this decision difficult to take. Some will walk away, finding it impossible. But others will respect the decision even though they disagree with it, and will be the first to support her, find her the best information and medical care, and ensure that she has all she needs, including people to care for her after the operation, as it's likely that she will be uncertain, fearful and vulnerable.

I believe, however, that it is important to educate men and women about the choices that are available, and to encourage them to choose life when it is at all possible. While supporting those who are facing difficult and painful decisions in a loving way, I want to be one of those who also speak up for the foetus, reminding people of his or her existence and that this little human being is more than just a complicating factor within our lives.

6 'What do you do?'

The question above serves several functions. It can be competitive, as we try and compare ourselves in the pecking order to the person we are talking to; it can be used to evaluate whether they are interesting or not and whether the conversation is worth continuing and it can be used, often unsubtly, by a parent to find out whether their child's boyfriend or girlfriend has got any prospects. It's a potent question and yet when we are asked it ourselves, we often end up mumbling the answer.

But it seems that we often get work the wrong way round. For some people, it is only a means to an end, the way in which they are able to feed themselves, go on holiday and buy a house. For others, if they are lucky, it is an investment of their gifts. Being good with their hands, they become craftsmen or being good at teaching, they go into education.

But whatever our take on work, we all have to deal with three fundamental questions which highlight a much deeper aspect to work than merely asking what do you do.

The first question is, 'what am I going to do with my life?' The second, asked in mid-life, is 'what am I doing with my life?' and the last, when we have reached retirement or at least a point where we can look back on what we have done, is 'what have I done with my life?'

These questions highlight two things: firstly that work is

another way of viewing life itself – it is not primarily about function but instead about journeying. Secondly, it is about how we use the life we have been given with its gifts, opportunities and constraints. This may not always seem to be the case when we do jobs that we do not like. But work can change us. It has the potential to become a transforming influence within our lives and the way in which we work has the power to transform society around us.

So starting work is like pushing a boat out into the sea. We have our lives ahead of us and we don't know how they're going to turn out. We don't know whether we are going to make a success of our lives, whatever that means, or whether we are going to live with disappointment. When we are young, we are promised a great deal. Schools attempt to prepare us to take our place in society and some of them do it better than others. But as we begin work, we are expressing something very deep about ourselves and perhaps begin to see that work is intertwined with our own spirituality.

Work, poverty and fulfilment

Not everybody is fulfilled in their job. Nor does work always pay enough to enable people to enjoy the benefits arising from a consumer society. In some cases, jobs may only pay enough to survive on, forcing people to live in areas where the social conditions are poor, the schools are under-resourced and with the constant threat of violence. In many places, there is high unemployment, a greater prevalence of poor health and those jobs that do exist are poorly paid. There is a cycle of deprivation from which it is difficult to escape. Going from one government agency to another for help saps the spirits until, eventually, the natural temptation is to give in and become a part of a culture where there is little incentive to find work, especially when it is so poorly paid and one is better off on benefits. Within this are people who do wish to work, having natural talents and gifts, who may once have been motivated, but are not only poor but powerless.

The situation can be even worse for those who are immigrants or refugees. They may find that although in their country of origin they had work that was rewarding, perhaps with professional status, when coming to another country, they are at the bottom of the pile. I know of one man who was a powerful entrepreneur in his own country and who had to flee because of threats made to his life. He is now living on unemployment benefits in appalling conditions, faces constant discrimination and has experienced significant periods of homelessness.

But millions of other people around the world have no work at all and little prospect of getting it through impoverished economies. So I accept that we cannot be sentimental about work. We know people are working extremely hard just to survive. We also know that contemporary slavery is on the increase, with young women especially being forced into prostitution or bonded labour. Young children are also often made to work in the most appalling circumstances, with their childhood quickly lost and, in many cases, a family depending on what they can earn.

It is clearly not the case, then, that all work is 'good work'. Some of it is 'bad work' and deeply oppresses the human spirit. And yet this oppression is one of the things which I believe highlights the potentially deeply spiritual nature of work. Christians believe that we were made by a God who is a worker and whose creativity is reflected in the extraordinary complexity and beauty of the universe. Although the world is not our possession (we did not make it), I would argue that it has been loaned to us to manage on God's behalf, given to us in trust. I think that we are beginning to see that we have abused that trust in the way we have had a negative impact on the world.

Work was originally intended to reflect God's desire that both we and the world should flourish. The fact that something has gone badly wrong in work is, therefore, a tragedy. Work is meant to be one of the many ways in which we can not only express ourselves creatively but through which we can both care for one another and enjoy the world. These things touch us deeply, both when they go wrong and when they work out for good since as we have seen, spirituality is essentially about who we are as human beings at the deepest level. It is about our bodies, our emotions, our thinking, as well as our relationship with God and with other people.

One of the key issues regarding work then is whether we feel fulfilled or not. Everybody wants to be fulfilled. We want to go to work feeling that what we are contributing is worthwhile, that we are being encouraged as human beings and that other people are benefiting from what we do. Work is also about belonging. Partly that is an expression of our desire to contribute to the community personally, but also it is part of our desire to belong to a community of workers who are contributing something positive to society.

But the meaning of work comes from something beyond work – some idea of where we're going. It's one of the reasons why we often get frustrated and leave a job saying, 'I'm worth more than this.' The higher the sense of our own personal worth, the more we need to feel that who we are can be expressed through what we do.

Our body can be present, then, but our heart is often elsewhere and we want to be investing in useful and worthwhile work.

Is ambition always good?

When we launch our boat on the sea of life, what is taking us forward? For many people, it is ambition. Rather than wanting a journey, they want a career, a well-defined path with key reference points along it where each one will bring greater rewards. They want a sense of security and an acknowledgment of status. But while there are many ambitious people around who may get their rewards, becoming well-known within their company or in the political arena for example, I believe that what really matters is who they are as people.

I've met people who had reached the end of their working lives and did not have friends or outside interests, whose family was unable to relate to them and, despite being chief executives of large companies, had become empty and lonely people. They had paid little or no attention to themselves, invested nothing in friendship and, in a way, had become lost.

> **I had a calling to become what I became, I was created to do this.**
> La Monte Young, composer

It's also possible to meet people who have been made redundant and yet can not admit that this has happened. There is a well-known true story about one man who got up at the same time every morning, put on his suit, caught the same train and walked around the City of London until

the time came to catch his usual train home. He
pretended that he had been at work all day. His whole life
was so bound up with his work that he could not even
admit to his wife that he was now unemployed.

But life and work seem very different when we think of
them as a 'calling'. This is a word that was once used far
more than it is today but I want to start a campaign for its
reinstatement! It has long been used to describe occupations
such as doctors, clergy and teachers, work that is seen as
going beyond just 'doing a job'. Such people might say
something like, 'I felt called to be a doctor,' or 'God is calling
me to be a missionary.' In its most profound sense, it places
work within a religious context because of who is doing the
calling. Originally such a person was saying, 'this is what
God wants me to do with my life' and I would argue that the
word makes most sense within this context.

> **Our mission is not just to make a
> profit, it is to fulfil a calling.**
> *Dianna Booher, entrepreneur and
> communications consultant*

Who you are, what you are doing and your very impact
on the world is summed up through your calling. You are
here for a purpose and it is not restricted to what you get
paid for, although that is part of it. Calling is about seeing
our lives as being integrated. It is about seeing the bigger
picture and it is about believing that whatever we are doing,
we are here for a purpose. Calling can be as much about the
humble as the grand things in life; as much about business
as religion. It can be serving customers as well as educating
children or healing patients.

'Calling' is a word for everyone – those doing all sorts of
work and who have invested in it something deep and

humane which we admire. As Martin Luther King once said in a speech in Kingston, Jamaica in 1965:

> *If it falls to our luck to be street sweepers, sweep the streets, like Raphael painted pictures, like Michelangelo carved marble, like Shakespeare wrote poetry and like Beethoven composed music. Sweep the streets so well that all the hosts of heaven and earth would have to pause and say... here lived a great street sweeper.*

So 'calling' is a word that should resonate deep within us. It is not only a statement about why we are here. It is also a far-reaching challenge about how far we are willing to go to change the world in which we live. Are we willing to take risks to conduct our business differently through the belief in our calling rather than cutting corners to maximise profits? Can we be bothered to make the effort to ensure the last shop customer of the day feels as welcome and valued as the first because we see this as part of our calling?

> **Every job is a self-portrait of the person who does it. Autograph your work with excellence.**
> *Unknown*

But seeing our life and work as a calling may not take us down a well-trodden or easy path. It's not the same as ambition because it's willing to let in all kinds of experiences that may, on the surface, be negative ones but which are essential if we are to see life as a journey and the world of work as one of the key ways through which we can be transformed.

Today, the world is crying out for people – especially young people – to invest their energy and vision in the world rather than living within their comfort zone. We cannot grow as human beings unless we are willing to take risks.

> **I submit to you that if a man hasn't discovered something he will die for, he isn't fit to live.**
> *Martin Luther King*

The gender agenda

Both men and women are able to enjoy the world of work today and there are few jobs that men do that women cannot do. However, there are still pay differentials between the sexes that are unjust and many women discover that there are glass ceilings, especially after having children. But for a moment, I want to look at the recent debates about the changing roles of men and boys.

At the beginning of the men's movement in the 1970s, American poet Robert Bly wrote *Iron John*, a modern interpretation of an old fable about a young boy who awoke a giant called Iron John. The story was about the impact of this on the boy and his picture of what is meant to be a man. In doing so, Bly highlighted that men are on many different kinds of journeys and that these change as one goes through life. He acknowledged that many young men carry burdens and experience delinquency and dysfunction. Their parents do not always prepare them for life or give them the tools or the sense of self-worth that they need to successfully navigate their way through life and enjoy it. But others, in Bly's own words, 'learn to fly'. They are the 'ascenders', the ones who have energy and are able to take off successfully, fuelled by desire, embracing all that life brings.

It's these kinds of men whom we all admire. They have characteristics that we wish to imitate, radiating energy and security, and living well beyond the mere functions of the work they do. Of course, this applies to both men and women and some of the most inspiring leaders in the world today are women. But over the last twenty years, people have been discussing the 'crisis in masculinity'. While women still face discrimination within their place of work, they perhaps have a momentum now that they did not have thirty years ago as society realises that there is little in the world of work which they cannot do.

Even those occupations which demand physical strength and which previously were thought to be the preserve of men are now changing as technology takes over from muscle power. However, what has also happened is that this has, indirectly, contributed to a crisis in male identity.

Some men point out that women have two sources of identity. The first is biological. Although some women cannot have children, it has traditionally been the case throughout the world that having children and raising a family has brought great dignity. The second is for women to use their gifts in the workplace, alongside men.

The reason why this may have contributed to a crisis in male identity, especially in the generation of men who have gone through the transition period in which many of these changes have taken place, is that traditionally men have only had one source of identity, which is in the world of work. Although fatherhood and being a husband is important to men, it has not always carried the same significance as motherhood has for women. It is not that men resent women entering the labour force; rather, it is that there is nothing now which is distinctive and which men can call their own. It is also the case that male leadership is becoming increasingly suspect in a world which is rapidly replacing hierarchy with networking.

It seems that many women today in the West are full of energy and hope, often being stretched in their workplace and enjoying the new opportunities that are opening up. However, some men today seem to be strangely lacking in energy.

> **My grandfather once told me that there were two kinds of people: those who do the work and those who take the credit. He told me to try to be in the first group; there was much less competition.**
> *Indira Gandhi*

This could be due to two things. First, as Bly said, the West has 'tamed' men and they have lost much of their energy as a result. Men are more uncertain about what they can do and what their role is in the new world of gender equality. In the world of work where men used to be at the top of a hierarchical system, many are today ill at ease with 'flat' networks where conversation, communication and relationship are important in forging efficient practices. But does this mean then that we should go back to the old ways? By no means! What it does mean, however, is that there are new tensions in the world of work that, although they may be resolved over time, need to be explored.

One friend who is a hospital doctor recently confirmed this. He told me that in his place of work, other doctors are struggling because his workplace had become increasingly relational. Many doctors, especially those who are senior, are finding it difficult to move from the old order of bureaucracy, hierarchy and committee game-playing to a more relational world in which conversation and the skilled handling of emotions is fast becoming a priority.

The second thing is a sense of 'numbness'. Many men find it difficult to express their feelings. Their inner world is often a foreign country and they have a restricted vocabulary with which to express their emotions. When I am asked to speak on masculinity, women often come up to me afterwards and ask 'how can I get my man to tell me what he's feeling? He seems embarrassed by the question but our relationship would be so much stronger if he could just tell me what's going on inside him.' This is slowly changing and younger men may find it easier to share what is going on in their heads but many men still find it difficult. Their world was traditionally the world of the functional, the world of the workplace. With that world being based around the male psyche, it ensured that men only needed a relatively limited emotional toolkit in order to maintain momentum and succeed.

So the new working practices and atmosphere sit uncomfortably with some men, especially those who are older. They feel that men have lost their distinctive role since women today can do everything that they can do. As a result, there is much uncertainty about male roles within the Western world and this is taking some time to work through. Hopefully, however, we will soon emerge into a world where men and women can both work and be parents together in an equal and mutually respectful partnership, one in which emotional, spiritual and practical aspects of character and gender can be integrated into a healthy concept of calling.

But what if everything goes wrong in life? I believe that one of the things about Christianity is that it never asks people to assess their lives by whether they believe they are a success or failure. It refuses to see life in such terms. At the heart of the Christian faith is a commitment of one's life to God and a positive acceptance of what life brings. This is not a passive acceptance, however, but instead an encouragement to see life as a pilgrimage and everything that we are and all that we have been given as resources for this pilgrimage. It also means that failures and even disasters that might befall us are important resources, as we can learn from them and possibly help others in time.

If God is with us, as I believe, then although we may become depressed because of the experiences that we are going through, God is able to use these experiences. For example, it is sometimes very difficult for people who have not experienced depression to sit alongside those who are currently going through it. Of course there are professionals and trained counsellors but in terms of friends, often the most helpful people are the ones who don't offer advice but instead stand with us in solidarity and are willing to share what they went through.

The Bible talks about the word 'redemption', by which it means that we can be liberated from the power of our wrongdoing and the influence of evil, by God. But one of the consequences of this is that whatever we go through can be used by God to bring about good. A period of apparent failure is unnerving to a person who is driven by ambition. If they are ill for too long, they may be overtaken by younger and fitter people; they have to work twice as hard to stay where they are on the ladder. But the person with the bigger picture in mind, whose life is fuelled by the desire to discover both what life is truly about, who they really are and who God is, is secure enough to know that sometimes a period of upheaval, failure or even grief is important in furthering this process.

Robert Bly talks about the ashes experience. This is when the rewards that we have been working for for so long turn to ashes in our mouth. Whether it is because of redundancy, illness or business failure or even the collapse of a relationship, we can quickly find ourselves feeling lost and alone, not sure where we are on the map that we had been following so carefully.

But the ashes experience can take us in two directions. First, it can be a time of defensiveness and denial, an unwillingness to face up to what has happened. Or secondly, it can be a time when we open ourselves up to the realisation that life is more than employment goals and what is happening is that we are being invited to switch from seeing work as a career to seeing life as a journey. This does not mean that our immediate experience is any less painful or that we may feel any less of a failure but it does mean that we might just be able to see that this is part of the bigger picture.

The back of the tapestry

One of the most vivid pictures of the hope that is at the heart of the Christian faith can be explained through the metaphor of a tapestry. When we ask what our lives are about and where we are heading, we often feel that we are facing the back of a tapestry. We can see that there are many colours represented there, can even see the knots which hold the thread in place, but we can't see the picture and find it difficult to understand what our life consists of.

The Christian hope is the belief that one day the tapestry will finally be turned round and we will see our lives as God has always seen them. For some of us there will be a great deal of darkness; we will have suffered and gone through stages in our lives which have been painful. But when we look at the tapestry from the front, we will be able to see how the whole picture makes sense and why it was necessary not to have seen it until a certain time, so that God was able to do what was necessary in our lives. So at the heart of the Christian faith there is a strong belief that for those who are committed to God, all things finally work together for good.

> **Pray as though everything depended on God. Work as though everything depended on you.**
> *St Augustine*

So as we start out looking at the world of work, we need to grapple with the fact that work is a deeply spiritual activity. If we are willing to look beyond what we are doing to the way in which we can ourselves be transformed by our attitudes to the world, we can in turn transform it for good.

7 The poverty of indifference

'Globalisation' is a good word to flash around at parties although we might find ourselves without friends if we do it too often! It's been one of the 'buzz' words for several years and is likely to remain so for several more to come. It describes the way in which our world is becoming increasingly interconnected. In the past, we used to use the word 'international' when wishing to look at the bigger picture but today we increasingly use the word 'global'. One of the reasons for this is that there are many issues that we face together, which are not resolvable between nations (inter-nationally). Instead they defy any kind of boundaries and we have to work on them co-operatively.

Pollution doesn't stop at a border, nor does crime, and today we face illness and even pandemics that are not contained within a particular country. We are now called to have a global imagination. Yet so many of the issues we have to deal with are negative ones that threaten to overwhelm us and we often end up wanting to listen to world music rather than contemplate world problems.

But if we can fight this urge to opt out and instead contribute something, helping in some way to resolve these issues, then we can feel like the mosquito in the quote further on in this chapter, knowing that we can all make an impact upon the world. As we saw in the chapter on work, the key issue is how we view both ourselves and the possibilities of what we can do with our life. I believe that indifference changes nothing except that we shrink a little as human beings.

Globalisation partly refers to the way in which financial markets are connected up and are operating 24/7. Billions of dollars are exchanged every day and some of them only stay in one place for a few seconds before being moved elsewhere in search of higher financial profits.

Technology today is also increasingly global, connecting us up so that we can use information, through the internet, which is stored on the other side of the world. And when we look at what we are wearing or open up our bags and look inside, it's very likely that we will find labels showing that the items come from many different areas of the world. Just looking round my study at the moment, I can see:

- books printed in China
- wooden shelves from Sweden
- a poster from France
- a computer from Korea
- a printer from Japan
- a guitar from Korea
- a pineapple juice carton from Spain
- a handbag from China (not mine)
- a leather jacket made in the UK.

Although the process of importing and exporting has been going on for many years, it is accelerating rapidly. Many may lose their jobs in the manufacturing industry in England due to decisions made thousands of miles away in boardrooms in Beijing. A car may be made with parts which come from twenty different nations. Businesses close down because it is cheaper to make the product in Asia where labour costs are much cheaper than in Europe where there are strict laws about minimum wages and health and safety.

I recently downloaded a new programme onto my computer called Google Earth. When you open it, you start in a position from space and quickly zoom in on any part of the world, even your own house. At the moment, some areas are very blurred because the photographs are not clear but in other parts of the world, the detail is extraordinary. You can type in names of hotels or leisure facilities and it will take you to them. The possibilities are endless!

In many senses, Google Earth is a powerful metaphor for the way in which we are now learning to see our world as a single entity. Those of us who wish to know more about the world can quickly do so and use it for our own interests but without realising that the more information we have about the world, the more responsibility we carry with it.

Make Poverty History

The Make Poverty History campaign brought together many hundreds of thousands of people, many of whom had never before given serious thought to the issues of debt, aid and trade, all of which were at the heart of the campaign. Dozens of organisations came together, communicating in a language that was easily understood and which explained the urgency of doing something to help people survive within the developing world.

The call was to take action by:

- lobbying the UK government at key events such as the G8 summit at Gleneagles
- joining public demonstrations to show the strength of feeling about injustice in areas such as debt, aid and trade
- buying a white wristband with 'Make Poverty History' stamped on it
- reading educational material and using it in schools and other groups
- financial giving to charities and aid agencies involved on the frontline
- looking at our personal history of consumer spending and the places that we travel to
- emailing local British MPs
- organising Make Poverty History events.

The idea was that a swell of support for the campaign would not only place immediate pressure on the world leaders who had the power to reduce debt and renegotiate trade regulations but that each individual participating would be empowered enough to believe they could make a difference.

> **If you think you're too small to be effective you've obviously never been in bed with a mosquito.**
> *Anon*

In a way, it's a modern interpretation of the story about a man who came across a small boy on a beach standing by an enormous pile of starfish that had just been washed up. The man asked the boy as he watched him throw them back one by one into the sea, 'what are you doing? Can't you see that there are millions of stranded starfish here? Leave them alone, you're wasting your time. It doesn't matter.' To which the boy replied, as he threw one more into the sea, 'it matters to that one.'

Mother Teresa once said, 'they say my work is just a drop in the ocean. I say the ocean is made up of drops.'

The Make Poverty History campaign was based around such a philosophy, teaching people the principle that we may not be able to do much individually about the extent of world poverty but we can do something within our own power. We can give money or time, write to politicians, join a demonstration or look at what we do when we visit other countries as a tourist, trying to ensure that when we leave, the people there have more dignity rather than less. We can even become volunteers and take a gap year, helping people who do not have the resources that the West has educationally, medically or through adequate housing.

Far from being powerless ourselves, the issue of poverty provides us with a host of opportunities to serve others in the world and by doing so ensure that our lives count for something more.

But it's also worth reminding ourselves not to give up on mainstream politics. Although some politicians invariably sound clichéd, weary and untrustworthy, that shouldn't be a reason to avoid politics entirely. Yet this is what most of us seem to be doing. The Royal Society for the Protection of Birds has more members than all the UK political parties put together!

In a recent MORI survey, figures showed that 7 per cent of young people between the ages of eleven and twenty-one had taken part in a demonstration against the war in Iraq. 23 per cent had boycotted a product for ethical reasons, 35 per cent had signed a petition and 9 per cent had written to a newspaper or taken part in a topical phone-in. However, 43 per cent of those who would be eligible to vote in the next UK general election said they would be very likely to use their vote.

Living with AIDS

Not all poverty is income poverty. Many people do not have access to education or nutritious food and are denied basic human rights. In some countries, women have such a low status that a back street industry booms in aborting girl foetuses. Millions are also dying through illnesses such as pneumonia, tuberculosis and HIV/AIDS. The latter is a global emergency and a major contributor to world poverty, with the vast majority of those people living with the effects of HIV/AIDS being from the developing world. Today, it's one of the biggest social, economic and health challenges facing us, claiming over 8,000 lives every day.

HIV stands for Human Immunodeficiency Virus. There are three ways that you can become infected (known as being HIV-positive). One is through unprotected sexual intercourse with an infected person. The second is through contact with an infected person's blood such as blood transfusions. However, in much of the world this is no longer a risk due to blood donations being routinely tested. But it can still be a risk if using illegal drugs through injection, as blood might be injected directly into the bloodstream through a needle. The third way is from a mother to her child, during pregnancy, birth or breastfeeding.

HIV breaks down the immune system, ensuring that it is more difficult to fight off infections. When a person then develops one or more of a number of serious illnesses, such as tuberculosis or pneumonia, as a result of the number of immune system cells left in their body falling below a particular level strong enough to fight back, they have acquired AIDS (Acquired Immune Deficiency Syndrome). At this stage, the body has very little defence against certain infections that can then prove deadly.

The time between HIV infection and having AIDS can be as little as a few years or more than a decade, depending on the person, their health and behavioural patterns. In 2005 there were over 40 million people around the world infected with the HIV virus including nearly 2.5 million children under the age of fifteen. Nearly 5 million others had become newly infected in 2005. In the UK, there are far fewer people dying of AIDS but HIV rates are nevertheless higher than ever before. Fortunately for those who live in fairly affluent societies, there is easy access to drugs which can delay the onset of AIDS by ten years or sometimes more. However, it remains a terminal illness.

Crisis and hope in Africa

AIDS has had a devastating social impact throughout the world but has perhaps become most associated with what is happening in Africa. Already nearly 26 million Africans are HIV-positive, constituting well over half the total number of infections worldwide. Unless something is done urgently, nearly 90 million Africans could be infected with HIV – 10 per cent of the continent's population – over the next twenty years.

But the devastating effect of HIV/AIDS is not just restricted to the continent of Africa. It's also expected to strike in the three most populous countries of the world – Russia, India, and China – over the next twenty-five years.

The economic costs within these three countries will also, arguably, be even greater than they have been in Africa given their rapidly burgeoning economies and status within the global economy.

> **Imagine if a third of the kids at your local primary school were AIDS orphans. That's a reality in Africa where the parents of 13 million children have been killed by AIDS.**
> *Bono*

The current statistics on Africa, however, overwhelmingly re-emphasise the links between poverty and AIDS. Poverty invariably leads to poor healthcare, education and nutrition. Poor health leads to time off work or even redundancy, ensuring that there are few means to provide for a family or to do anything except survive. It also ensures that for most families affected in some way by HIV/AIDS, they do not have the money to invest in the drugs needed for survival.

Through the ravaging effects of AIDS, Africa is losing thousands of farmers, engineers, teachers, doctors, mothers and fathers every day, and there are already more than 12 million orphaned children who live in sub-Saharan Africa. And yet, despite all this, there are some positives to report on.

A few countries within Africa have seen their adult HIV prevalence rates (the proportion of adults living with HIV) decline, for various reasons. Uganda, for example, saw its HIV rates drop considerably, largely through its government's policies. These were credited with helping to bring the number of those infected down from around 15 per cent in the early 1990s to 5 per cent in 2001. At the end of 2003, it was estimated that only 4 per cent of adults had the virus.

This was largely due to persistent educational campaigns and easy access to healthcare. Effective communication perhaps, however, played the biggest role, especially at the grass-roots level and with those already HIV-positive leading the campaign. This helped to break down the stigma that had built up around the virus and ensured also that open discussions about sex could be had, previously a taboo subject.

Unlike a lot of African countries at the time, Uganda quickly recognised the dangers of HIV/AIDS and took swift action to prevent the spread of the virus, using the above strategies and also its population as 'messengers' to spread the word and to work together. In doing so, they brought the issue out into the open and reduced the level of fear that was operating.

knowing the ABC

One of the key issues that the Ugandan government implemented was the ABC method:

- Abstain from sex
- Be faithful
- Use a condom.

First adopted by the Botswana government in the late 1990s, it was taken up by the Ugandan government soon after. As a result, young people started to have sex at a later age and people generally had fewer sexual partners, encouraged as they were to not have casual sex but, instead, stay with a regular partner. The government used the term 'zero grazing' to describe this. The people of Uganda also became educated about using condoms wherever possible.

According to one expert on HIV/AIDS, the effect of the prevention strategy in Uganda, and particularly the reduction in the number of sexual partners in the 1990s, had a similar impact to a vaccine that was 80 per cent successful.

Today, more and more countries around the world are starting to accept the fact that if they are to avert a major AIDS crisis, they must take speedy action.

> **AIDS obliges people to think of sex**
> **as having, possibly, the direst**
> **consequences: suicide. Or murder.**
> *Susan Sontag*

As we've seen in a previous chapter, it's important to come to terms with the significance of sex in our lives. I believe that we need to see sex as far more than just a recreational activity and instead as a deep expression of who we are and with wholehearted respect for the person with whom we are making love. In other words, we need to ask the question, 'is practising safe sex enough?' It may stop the transmission of an STD but when you hear a thirteen-year-old girl asking, 'what does it matter? It's only sex,' just maybe it's time to stop and think about where we have got to in our society.

Human rights and human slavery

Human rights is another issue of enormous global significance. There are two kinds of rights: positive rights – rights to have something that enables you to survive or to flourish as a human being, such as education; and negative rights – rights to not have something done to you, such as torture or the refusal to allow you freedom of expression. These have been called 'freedom from want' and 'freedom from fear'.

Every person has rights just by virtue of being born. Whoever they are. Whatever they have done. However much we dislike them. The fact that we all have certain basic rights, regardless of what we have done personally, is one of the foundations of a civilised society.

Every right, however, entails a responsibility. If someone says that they have a right to something the issue is, who has a responsibility to give it to them? It might be another person who owes them money and who should pay it back or it might be the national government which has pledged to provide education but instead is defaulting on its promises.

In some cases, national governments will become corrupt and will use torture and other similar methods to maintain order within society. One of the major scandals of the twenty-first century is that Western armies, including the British and the US, have been found guilty of torturing prisoners, particularly in the Abu Ghraib prison in Iraq.

Women, children and disabled people can often be left utterly powerless and without a voice, with their rights ignored. In some countries, women do not even have the right to say 'no' to a man who wishes to have sex with them, often ensuring that they have another child regardless of whether they want this.

In some cases, largely due to local superstitions, older men believe that through having sex with a young girl, they will be cured of having the HIV virus. Often, a man will give such a girl small amounts of money for school books in order to lower her resistance. In other situations, and as has been seen recently in various wars, young children are forced into becoming child soldiers, with all the horror and trauma that that entails.

Perhaps the most hidden form of the denial of human rights is through contemporary slavery. This does not include people who work in sweatshops or those suffering from absolute poverty. Instead, slaves are controlled by violence, usually physical in nature, by being shackled or maimed to prevent them escaping; they cannot walk away from their job and are always held against their will. They are paid nothing.

> **There are more slaves alive today than all the people stolen from Africa in the time of the transatlantic slave trade.**
> **Put another way, today's slave population is greater than the population of Canada and six times greater than the population of Israel.**
> *Kevin Bales*

At the beginning of the twenty-first century, the price of a slave is at its lowest ever. According to Kevin Bales, one of the world experts on slavery, the average slave costs around US$100. He refers to them as 'disposable people' because they are so cheap that when they are exhausted or ill and of no use to those who are exploiting them, they can be turned out on the street or disposed of in more sinister ways. Several factors have contributed to this growth in contemporary slavery. There has, for instance, been a large population explosion in the developing world. Also the replacement of subsistence farming by cash crops, has led to a major increase in the slums and shanty towns of many cities. Then there is the rapidly increasing existence of corrupt policing and governments that turn a blind eye to the most important element in any form of slavery – violence.

Estimates of the number of slaves in the world range from Bales' conservative estimate of 27 million up to 200 million. The reason for such uncertainty is because, like an iceberg, slavery is nearly always contained below the surface.

Liberation for the oppressed?

Slavery takes many forms. It is estimated that 20 million people are bonded slaves, meaning that they are forced to work for an employer to whom they owe money. The arrangement often means, however, that it is virtually impossible for them to reach the point when the debt or the loan can be paid back. This means that they cannot get out.

Children are also deeply affected by slavery. According to Anti-Slavery International, the oldest human rights organisation (founded in 1787) and one of the groups that is at the forefront of the fight against slavery:

- 179 million are estimated to work through the worst forms of child labour – one in eight of the world's five-to seventeen-year-olds

- 111 million children under fifteen are employed in hazardous work
- 8.4 million children are in slavery, trafficking, debt bondage and other forms of forced labour, forced recruitment for armed conflict, prostitution, pornography and other illicit activities
- 50,000 women and children are trafficked into the US every year for sexual exploitation.

The most horrific and well-known example of contemporary slavery may well be the enslavement of the Dinkas in Southern Sudan. According to U.S. State Department estimates, up to 90,000 are owned by North African Arabs, and are often sold as property in a thriving slave trade for as little as $15 per human being.

> **Slavery... I didn't know about all these forms that existed. I think it's largely because we aren't expecting it. It is hidden. Generally people would not believe that it is possible under modern conditions. They would say 'No, I think you are making it all up', because it's just too incredible...**
> *Archbishop Desmond Tutu*

One of the most positive things that Christianity has been responsible for, socially, over the past 200 years is the anti-slavery movement in the eighteenth and nineteenth centuries. It was led by Christians such as William Wilberforce, and which brought about the eventual abolition of the slave trade.

But while legal ownership of slaves has been abolished,

control by force has not. Unfortunately there is little evidence that Christians are as committed today as they were in Wilberforce's day to this new fight, a trade that feeds off a globalised world economy. It is a world in which women and children are trafficked against their will across borders into areas of work such as prostitution and pornography.

But whatever we may feel personally, I believe that we are not powerless against such forces and instead should join with others such as NGOs (Non-Government Organisations) as well as those organisations that are focused exclusively on modern slavery. In doing so, we can ensure that we become more educated about the issues and able to devote time and money to the cause as well as emailing our political representatives.

Such effort will, inevitably, lead to us becoming more passionate and more informed about the world, knowing that we have made a difference to the world in which we live.

So whenever we look closely at the issue of poverty, we realise with horror that poverty is not just concerned with 'income poverty' but also concerned with human poverty. It is about a lack of opportunity and a restriction of choice that dehumanises people and ensures they cannot survive with any kind of quality of life.

In a globalised world, many people are information rich but many more are information poor. The fact that you are reading this book and I have written it means that it's likely we are information rich, giving us extraordinary opportunities to help those who cannot help themselves. It also means that when the question is asked, 'who takes the responsibility to help those who are in need?' we must be willing to play our part, put our hands up and say, 'me.'

caring for the earth

Most of us are aware that there is widespread concern
about the future of the planet, whether it is in the
encroaching of deserts on fertile land, the purity of the
water that we drink, deforestation, the acidification of
oceans or massive climate change. We are faced with a
bewildering catalogue of situations where it seems that not
only is the future bleak but that the issues are so huge that
we are seemingly powerless to affect the situation.

Deep within many of us is a sense that the world cannot
be taken for granted. Whatever we believe about its origins,
whether they are most accurately described by the theory
of evolution or whether the purpose of the earth's existence
is best captured through the story of creation in Genesis,
we have within us the conviction that the world is a gift. Of
course this raises the issue about who is the giver but
whatever our beliefs, it is difficult to escape, I believe, from
this innate sense that it has been given to us in order to be
celebrated. It is something that we should be thankful for.

And yet alongside this comes the knowledge that
although the planet may indeed be a gift, it is not ours to
possess. It is not ours to do with as we wish. It is more
like a loan given to us for the duration of our lives and, as
such, carries grave implications in our attitude towards it.

First, we are responsible for it. One of the reasons why
we are in difficulties environmentally is that we have
carelessly used the world and its resources without
thinking either about whether our actions are for the good
of the planet or about whether the consequences of such
actions will be destructive. Frequently in the past, we have
treated the world's resources as if they were limitless and
the world's oceans and its air as if they could absorb

anything that we threw at them. We have found to our cost that this is not so. We are now aghast at what we have done to the planet and are beginning to realise that we are the most rapacious species on the planet, by far.

So we are very slowly and sometimes reluctantly trying to recover our sense of responsibility for the planet in which we live, personally, corporately and socially. And we are not powerless in bringing about this change.

As shown previously within this book, we can do many things. We can apply pressure on those who are in power to bring about change. We can add our weight and lend our personal resources to action groups that campaign on our behalf. We can protest against those multinationals and smaller corporations whose presence is destructive rather than creative. And we can examine our own lifestyle, asking whether there are issues that we should face up to and which carry personal implications for us.

The second issue that many people feel is a sense of accountability or rather a lack of it. But the question here is, to whom are we accountable? Of course we are accountable to one another for our actions. We live within the rule of law; we regulate behaviour so that, for example, a factory may not discharge pollution into a river without legal consequences. But I think that this sense of accountability goes deeper than that, because it is generated by the sense of longing which is at the heart of so many of the issues that we have been looking at in this book. There is in each of us, I believe, a longing not only to be spiritually whole as people but for the wholeness of the earth.

Responsibility and accountability

In the book of Genesis, the creation story describes an aftermath that shows the implications of man and woman disobeying God, preferring to make their own decisions rather than trusting God's way as the best. By doing that, of course, Adam and Eve (who in the story represent all men and women) cut themselves off from God. There were also implications for their own relationship, which became characterised by the man dominating the woman rather than having the equality that God had intended. Work also changed from being a joy to being difficult and, in some cases, oppressive. The world had changed and the fruitfulness of the earth was compromised so much that the world itself was no longer the place that God had intended it to be.

Of course we can still see the beauty of the world, in people and their relationships, and we can still enjoy 'good work'. In other words, God's original intentions for the world have not fully disappeared. But we are also aware of the pain, ugliness, pollution and injustice that were never intended to be there. As I have written previously, Christians believe that we are accountable to God as well as to one another for what we do with this world as well as what we have done with the lives that we have been given and the resources we own.

This is sombre stuff and yet this sense of responsibility and accountability needs to be tempered with the joy, celebration and sense of blessing that we often feel, especially when we are struck by the beauty of the world around us. There can be few people who have walked on snowy mountains or in beautiful countryside, or even sat on rocks with the sea crashing around them and not found growing within them an inexplicable sense of awe and celebration.

I think that this is not only part of the sense of longing that is at the heart of every person but it taps into the desire to worship and to see nature as part of a much larger creation. Perhaps even having the knowledge that what we see all around us is evidence of something much bigger than ourselves being in control, whose goodness can be seen in every blade of grass as well as in the stars that we were gazing at in the first chapter.

It is the merging then of celebration and a sense of responsibility that forms the bedrock of our response to the environment. We will all make our personal response in different ways but it is increasingly important that each of us discovers at least one way to ensure that we don't just leave the earth as we found it but that having lived our lives, the earth is in a better state than it would have been if we had never existed. The fact that this can be true for everybody reading this book should both excite us and give us a sense of hope, knowing that we can contribute not only to the quality of life of other people but to the very planet that I believe we have been given as a gift from God.

8 'Be afraid, be very afraid'

This quotation from David Cronenburg's 1986 film *The Fly* conveniently sums up one of the key themes of the twenty-first century. At the same time as some of us are emphasising our freedom of choice within a consumer society and our enjoyment of human rights within a Western democracy, we are also struggling with fear. This tide of fear is rising, through the increase of terrorism, environmental changes such as global warming, health pandemics such as AIDS and even the possibility of catching avian (bird) flu. The standard of living within the West has never been so high and yet we still feel fragile and vulnerable. Coupled with this is the fact that we are not sure of whether to feel proud of what we have achieved.

There is no doubt that we live in a violent age and the twenty-first century has brought with it new forms of violence. Violence changes all of us. It is the intention of a violent person to provoke a response of sorts within us and yet there are three possibilities that we can choose in terms of our own response.

First, we can opt for indifference. While violence is directed at other people, we can sit back and do nothing about it. We blame others for perpetrating the violence and we blame governments for not doing enough to defend us against it. But indifference is not just the absence of involvement. It is also an emotional response that refuses to engage with the suffering of other people both in our own society and elsewhere in the world.

Of course, it's easy to become numb to this, having watched blanket TV coverage of the impact of violence in places such as Iraq and Afghanistan. But people who are indifferent find it difficult to rise above this, and do not see the implications for themselves in what is going on.

Secondly, we can opt for oppression. For example, an increasing number of people in the UK have joined organisations and movements that stereotype people from minority ethnic groups and, by doing so, add to the breakdown of multicultural society. Oppressors see others as the source of violence and their own actions as self-righteous and justified. Whether it is a playground bully, a violent husband or a member of a far-right political organisation such as the British National Party, oppressors deal in fear and seek to dehumanise people in order to gain power for themselves and for their beliefs.

Thirdly, we can be peacemakers. I go into more detail on this at the end of this chapter but in essence, this is the true calling of any person who wishes to be whole and to celebrate humanity in all its varieties. Of course, many Christians would argue that becoming a soldier is an honourable way of being a peacemaker, while others will find this impossible to accept.

Some will want to claim that there is such a thing as a just war and others will state that all wars are unjust. And certainly religion has been at the heart of many conflicts, with many people committing violent and unjust acts in its name. For instance, whenever someone wants to go to war for whatever motive and cites religion as the reason or claims that God has told them to go to war, then we know we are in real trouble.

But others have followed the call to become peacemakers and have brought healing to a fractured world. This can take many forms. Some have gone as medical missionaries into high-risk environments in order to bring education and healthcare to places where before they did not exist. Others have been willing to be conciliators between warring factions. Others still have become church leaders in urban priority areas where violence is never far from their own front door.

To be a peacemaker then is to build community rather than destroy it, to opt for understanding and love rather than indifference and oppression and is yet another way of expressing the spiritual that lies within us. It is no coincidence that the symbol used by Christians for the Holy Spirit is a dove of peace and that one of the key hallmarks of Christian character is peace. The apostle Paul links the internal peace that many Christians have through their focus on 'all that is good' with the external peace that they seek to bring to fractured communities around the world.

A twenty-first century challenge

The world was fundamentally changed by the events of September 11 2001 (or 9/11) in New York. Before then, many had had a fragile sense of optimism about the world, seeing the Berlin Wall falling in 1989, the Cold War over soon after, only one superpower remaining and no likelihood of a major new worldwide confrontation as evidence of a new consensus within the world.

For many people then, it came as a real shock to discover that there was another form of war that could threaten a country like the United States within its own borders. The US had previously thought of itself as untouchable, as although it had gone through the War of Independence and the Civil War, no nation had ever

managed to invade its land or even attack it from the air.

The events of 9/11 changed all that. It was frightening for several reasons. First, the United States realised that it was up against an invisible enemy. Anybody could be a terrorist. We could be sitting next to somebody on a plane or in the subway or even live next door to them and not know that their intention is to wreak havoc on the lives of innocent people.

Secondly, the question began to be asked, what motivated the terrorists? Many people in the West could not get inside the heads of such people. But perhaps this inability to understand what had gone wrong was the one thing that struck fear into the hearts of so many. Why would anyone kill thousands of law-abiding innocent people? Why would they also take their own lives in doing so? Were they mad? The most startling conclusion, however, was that they were not mad. Instead, they were intelligent people who had planned this campaign meticulously and saw its completion as an act of war to be celebrated.

> **Imagining what it is like to be someone other than yourself is at the core of our humanity. It is the essence of compassion, and it is the beginning of morality.**
> *Ian McEwan writing after 9/11*

Many people who knew nothing about Islam before 9/11 were quickly willing, unfairly, to stereotype it as a religion of violence. The twin towers had fallen and with them the American dream seemed to be turning into a nightmare.

Thirdly, the hatred that had rapidly fuelled terrorism was

largely directed at the West and, in particular, at America. But many Americans found it difficult to understand why such hatred was directed at them when they saw themselves as having had a positive or at least benign influence on the world.

And yet America has largely been an insular nation with much of its population not following events in the rest of the world in any sort of detail. It also has a natural confidence in its own actions, both domestically and abroad, believing them to be right and proper. Sadly, it is not the case for millions of people around the rest of the world who have suffered from the attention of the CIA in propping up various military regimes against the will of local populations, the American military presence in Saudi Arabia and its paranoid and disastrous presence in the Vietnam War. It is understandable then that many people throughout the world do not see America as a benign influence or as a country that has only ever sought to spread democracy throughout the world.

What are we afraid of?

The word 'terrorist' comes from the word *terrere,* which means 'to cause to tremble'. The emphasis then is not only on what the terrorist does but also on its impact on the public imagination. From this perspective, the events at the World Trade Center on 9/11 were one of the most effective acts of terrorism the world had ever seen. America's imagination was transformed. On the one hand, it became more defensive and nervous about its obvious vulnerabilities but on the other hand, it saw itself as the greatest military power in the world, giving it the right to crush those who used terror to intimidate innocent people.

In his response to the events of 9/11, George W. Bush even went so far as to describe America's retaliation as 'a crusade'.

> **I went to the airport to check in and they asked what I did because I looked like a terrorist. I said I was a comedian. They said, 'say something funny then.' I told them I had just graduated from flying school.**
> *Ahmed Ahmed*

And not surprisingly, terrorism did not end with the events of 9/11. Countries such as Kenya, Indonesia, Spain, Turkey, England and Sri Lanka have all felt the impact of the terrorist threat since then. And the name al-Qaeda has today become synonymous with a shadowy network of people that has few distinguishing features other than a hatred for the West and, in many cases, a desire to bring about an Islamist state.

This raises two issues. First, is it realistic to believe that the war on terror can ever be won? It seems difficult to imagine how something that is invisible, incoherent and fuelled by the willingness of so many to be martyred can ever be eradicated. It is easy to put a city on red alert and to have thousands of intelligence operatives searching for people who may be suspects but recent events in London, Madrid and elsewhere show how easy it is for a small group of individuals to cause chaos and bring about destruction and death. One of the issues facing the twenty-first century generation is, then, how to live with this constant threat of terrorism.

Secondly, is the process of trying to win the war on terror going to ensure that democracy will be damaged? It is convenient to argue that terror suspects should be treated differently from other criminals and be denied the right of trial by jury or even to believe that it's right for them to be kept for many days without access to trial, often not knowing what they are accused of. But is there not a danger in this, claiming that as we are living with unprecedented dangers, this therefore calls for unprecedented action? It is very easy once this has been accepted to change the law to such an extent that human rights are constrained or even curtailed. I would argue, however, that it is an empty victory if in ridding the world of terrorists we instead create an oppressive society.

The United States, for example, has been holding several hundred terror suspects at Guantanamo Bay in what are, according to human rights organisations, appalling conditions and in circumstances where they are denied even basic human rights. Whether Guantanamo is shut down in the near future or not, it highlights how a commitment to democracy, even at the highest levels, can quickly become compromised through feeling threatened by outsiders.

> **When citizens of democracy insist that what matters most in a terrorist emergency is the safety of the majority, they are usually saying that rights are at best a side constraint, at worst a pesky impediment to robust and decisive action.**
> *Michael Ignatieff*

The question is whether terrorism is more about war or politics. Perhaps it is best to say that it is about 'violent politics'. If so, it cannot just be fought by weapons but must also be fought through persuasion and argument. This can be seen through the recent war in Iraq where the Allies overwhelmingly won the military battle but found that in doing so, they had alienated much of the population and created the conditions in which terrorism could flourish. The Allies, it seems, had not won the 'hearts and minds' of the people.

> **The terrible thing about terrorism is that ultimately it destroys those who practise it. Slowly but surely, as they try to extinguish life in others, the light within them dies.**
> *Terry Waite*

The role of religion

It's difficult to believe now that only a few years ago many people felt that religion had declined in power to such an extent that it could no longer exert any influence on the world stage. In fact, the opposite has been true. The main tensions in the world today seem to be religious and cultural.

Since religion is about ultimate values and meaning, and is tied up with people's personal identity and view of their eternal destiny, then it is capable of motivating both terrorists and peacemakers. It is important, therefore, to ask fundamental questions about how so much of the violence currently perpetrated by terrorists is supposedly inspired by religious convictions.

In the popular imagination, we see the new conflict as being not between communism and capitalism but instead between Islam and the West. This is unfortunate because at its heart, Islam is a peaceful religion in which most people wish to coexist with one another in a mutually beneficial way. There are, of course, tensions between different ethnic and religious groups and, in Iraq, tensions between the Shia majority and the Sunni minority. But the people who are creating the problems here are not Muslims per se but instead Islamists, those who have created an ideology out of Islam which they seek to impose on others, believing it to be true in absolute terms. Because of such beliefs, almost anything seems to be justified in bringing about such a vision for society – including terrorism.

One of the problems is, however, that when terrorists are seen to be Muslims, or even people with another skin colour or ethnic background, then tolerance is put under strain in the society which is being attacked. The majority of people involved are innocent, however, and have nothing to do with terrorism. They just look as if they could come from the same ethnic or religious background. Because of this, they often have to face insults, abuse and the threat of physical attack as the fear and anger of a society spills over in its bid to find a target. When this becomes a regular event, then terrorism has begun to succeed, through a free society being placed under threat.

If a terrorist attack is associated with Islam, then our commitment to one another in a pluralistic society will need to be stronger and our friendships closer if they are to withstand the stress that terrorism brings to mixed communities.

I would argue strongly that this is no time for Christians to fuel the flames of fear by stereotyping members of other faiths negatively and emphasising the many differences between us as humans. What is important is that without denying the Christian belief in the uniqueness of Jesus Christ, Christians affirm the rights of other faiths to coexist

in a multicultural society and find common areas of
agreement that can be mutually affirmed.

The call to become peacemakers

The word 'fundamentalist' is often used in association with
terrorism and, in this sense, means those who believe in
something which is true in absolute terms. In other words,
they believe that they are right, that others are wrong and
that they have the right to impose their beliefs on others
because they are wrong. All religions have their
fundamentalists, whether it be Christianity, Judaism, Islam
or Hinduism. Some Christians, for instance, have bombed
abortion clinics, believing that those doctors who carried
out abortions were committing evil and deserved to die. In
the Middle East, suicide bombers have entered cafés or
buses and blown up many dozens of people, believing that
in doing so they would receive reward in the afterlife and
be remembered not as murderers but as martyrs.

Whether it is through the dogma of some of the Northern
Ireland churches or through the distorted interpretation of
Scripture by right-wing churches in South Africa,
sectarianism and violence can go hand in hand when fuelled
by a fundamentalist worldview. Dialogue can easily fail when
one is talking to someone who believes not only that they
are right but also that they have God on their side.

> **In violence we forget who we are.**
> *Mary McCarthy*

However, it's not always the case that religion is linked
to violence and terrorism. It can also give rise to
peacemaking, even if this is often a high-risk strategy when

dealing with situations of conflict. Pope John Paul II once called for people in such situations to make 'audacious gestures of peace' and such acts can be carried out by people from all religious backgrounds as well as none. But it is urgent and important that all those who have a religious faith spend time thinking through how that faith can be reflected by being peacemakers – even in a small way – in a violent world.

I believe, then, that Christians are called to be peacemakers, whether this is done informally, as mediators in disputes between friends or neighbours, or whether it is done formally, through becoming a government peacekeeper or professional mediator. The call to be a peacemaker goes back to Jesus' own example and his call in the book of Luke, chapter six, to love our enemies and do good to those who hate us. His famous call to turn the other cheek when we are struck shows the extent to which he expects Christians to expose violence by not retaliating.

Throughout history, Christians have divided into two types: pacifists, who will not use violence under any circumstances, even to defend themselves, and those who believe that there are conditions in which war can be just. But even here, Christians are called to commit to peacemaking, and war should only ever be used as a last resort, after everything else has been tried, and when peace is the likely result of such a war. It should be declared by the proper authorities, there should be discrimination between combatants and non-combatants and only sufficient force should be used to attain an objective. This does not exhaust the list of constraints on the conduct and declaration of war if it is to be considered just but some would say that such principles can never apply to a war fought with modern technology.

Others would ask how one intends to apply such

principles to a situation characterised by guerrilla warfare. Whatever the situation, we are only too aware that many wars throughout history have unfortunately not measured up to such high ideals, even those involving so-called Christians.

Peace is more powerful than violence because of the latter being a temporary display of human wilfulness. Christians see violence as one day coming to an end through the brutal death of Christ absorbing the violence of the world; past, present and future violence defeated through the resurrection. It is true that we still live in a violent age but at the heart of the Christian faith there is a strong belief that a new world is coming in which there will be no war or violence and in which, in the words of the prophet Isaiah, 'the lion will lie down with the lamb'.

With such a vision, there is ultimately no need to be fearful because if death itself has been defeated by Christ, as I believe, then it becomes the opening of a door into a new world.

9 Forgiveness is for losers

The title of this chapter is the name of one of 2005's most popular car racing computer games. It comes with the advice, 'fight dirty or go down in flames.' One guide says that the aim is to 'learn how to exact revenge on your fellow motorists in the worst way possible'. Given the amount of suppressed anger on many of our roads already, perhaps the game is meant to offer some kind of therapy for those who would otherwise exact revenge on a real road. It is more likely, however, that it is some kind of practice run.

'I'll get you back if it's the last thing I do', is a familiar playground promise to which the brave riposte is sometimes, 'oooh, you and whose army?'

When we are hurt by others, it is easy to either run away, keep quiet, excuse it or even collude with it in order to find some way of reducing its power in our lives. It is also easy to retaliate by attacking those who have wronged us. Together, they form the classic fight or flight syndrome, basic instincts that are finely honed in the school playground and sharpened further in the competitive world in which many of us live and work.

And it's difficult to forgive those who have abused us in some way. Perhaps this is because it seems so irrational to do so. Isn't forgiving people tantamount to letting them off the hook?

People who forgive

On Wednesday 29 April 2005, 26-year-old Abigail Witchalls was walking down a country path in the English county of Surrey with her 21-month-old son Joseph, when she was chased, stabbed in the neck and left for dead. Her injuries ensured that she was paralysed from the neck down. The attacker also held a knife to Joseph's neck. The police closed the case after the man who was most likely to have committed the crime committed suicide ten days after the attack.

Before it was known what had happened to her attacker, during an interview with Fiona Bruce on the BBC TV programme *Crimewatch*, her husband Benoit said, 'maybe the reason I'm here talking to you is so that this person can be found and something can be done to help them in some way. We haven't had any feelings of anger; it's just a case of helping out this person, really.' Then on hearing of the death of Abigail's suspected attacker, Richard Cazaly, her father extended their sympathy and prayers to the Cazaly family for their loss.

This act of forgiveness by the Witchalls family, all devout Roman Catholics, was remarkable and sparked a great deal of media comment, with journalists recording how refreshing it was to find a 'genuine' act of Christian goodness. Another remarkable thing was the spirit of the family itself, which refused to succumb to bitterness. Benoit said, 'we feel very lucky and very blessed because she is fully present as herself. It's just great to see and it's a great joy. You can see in her face when she sees Joseph. The reason that the first word she mouthed was "happy" was because she was so relieved that he came out of it unscathed, physically.' Even when

Abigail was still in her hospital bed, she said, 'God is doing beautiful things' – a comment that seemed breathtaking when compared to any rational perception of her situation.

Two months later, on 29 July 2005, British student Anthony Walker was murdered in a vicious attack that was both premeditated and racially motivated. He was found with an axe in his head. The two young men convicted of his murder were aged seventeen and twenty. Gee Walker, his mother, forgave his killers with these words, 'at the point of death, Jesus said: "I forgive them, they don't know what they do." I've got to forgive them – I still forgive them. My family and I stand by what we believe – forgiveness.'

> **To forgive is to set a prisoner free and discover that the prisoner was you.**
> *Lewis B. Smedes*

If it were impossible to forgive, then evil would have won the day. What painful and costly forgiveness did, as shown by both the Witchalls and Walker families, was to show those who perpetrated violence and the community in general that there was another power at work, another way of living life which did not depend on more violence and yet which could change the world. In essence, they lifted a burden from the guilty for what seemed to be entirely irrational reasons. But as a result, the ripples of their actions spread throughout the world.

'I forgive you'

On 8 June 1972, during the Vietnam War, children and
their families fled the village of Trang Bang down Route 1,
their bodies seared by napalm. The image of one young girl
naked and screaming was particularly etched onto the
world's collective memory through the photography of
Huynh Cong 'Nick' Ut, an AP photographer. The girl's
name was Phan Thi Kim Phuc.

The *Observer* newspaper described the photograph as
'the most haunting image of the horror of war since Goya'.
In the *International Herald Tribune*, Tom Buerkle wrote,
'for anyone old enough to remember the Vietnam War, the
photograph of the naked nine-year-old girl running toward
a camera screaming in agony as napalm burned her flesh
is seared into the consciousness. Her image has become a
symbol of war that transcends debate about the rights or
wrongs of U.S. intervention in Vietnam.'

She needed seventeen operations and her body today still
bears the scars of her suffering. But now as a Canadian
citizen, she has become a goodwill ambassador for
UNESCO. As a Christian, she learned the power of
forgiveness both for herself and for others as she sat on her
own in a little church in Saigon. Instead of feeling bitterness
towards those who nearly destroyed her life, she has forgiven
those responsible for her injuries.

At a ceremony commemorating the Vietnam War in
Washington, she told an audience of veterans that if she
were to meet with the pilot who had dropped the bomb
that caused such horrific injuries, 'I would tell him we
cannot change history, but we should try to do good things
for the present and for the future to promote peace.' John
Plummer, one of those who co-ordinated the attack on

Trang Bang, was in the audience. She welcomed him with
open arms.

In a subsequent interview with the UNESCO press she
said:

> *I have lived with my pain; I know the value of love
> when you want to heal. I have lived with hatred, and
> now I know the power of forgiveness. Today, I am alive,
> I live without hatred, without the spirit of revenge, and
> I can tell all those who caused my suffering: I forgive
> you. That is the only way to save peace, to speak of
> tolerance and non-violence. To have wrong done to you
> and not to forgive makes you a victim rather than
> someone who can bring about change for the better.*

An act of liberation

Forgiveness is an act of liberation for those who forgive and for those who are forgiven. It doesn't sweep the wrongdoing under the carpet but instead calls on both sides to look at what has been done in the cold light of day. But the remarkable thing is, and this is where the whole thing begins to look quite absurd, true forgiveness does not wait for an apology. It is not a magnanimous response to someone saying, 'I'm sorry for what I have done', to which we respond, 'OK I forgive you,' although things can sometimes happen that way. No, forgiveness is innovative. It is risk-taking behaviour. It is willing to go out on a limb and create the climate in which people can, if they want, change their attitude. Of course they may not, but by refusing they will have missed out on responding positively to our offer of forgiveness.

> **Once a woman has forgiven her man, she must not reheat his sins for breakfast.**
> *Marlene Dietrich*

What happens if we take the huge step of forgiving someone and then they turn around and tell us where we can stick our forgiveness? They are, in effect, 'preferring darkness to light', as the Bible suggests. We cannot force people to accept forgiveness. We can tell them that they are forgiven but if they reject it, this forgiveness cannot then act as a liberating force within their lives and loses its power to transform. Nevertheless, that act of forgiveness should never be withdrawn. As far as we are concerned, it should always be on offer.

But the other act of liberation that arises from forgiveness is summed up really well by the apostle Paul in one of his letters to the churches. He wrote, 'love keeps no record of wrongs.' In other words, if we forgive somebody we agree to 'wipe the slate clean'. Of course it is difficult to erase the memory of what has happened but we choose not to bring it up or let it prejudice our relationship with that person in the future. It is one of the things that is so crucial at the heart of any marriage or indeed any relationship. If one or both partners keep a record of all the things that their partner has said and done to them are is hurtful, then the relationship will sooner or later either fall apart or quickly become a sham. Forgiveness wipes the slate clean. Every day is a new day.

By now it should be apparent what a radical action forgiveness is. Yet we rarely see forgiveness displayed in such powerful terms. Most of us are only aware of a pale imitation of the real thing. I believe that the lack of forgiveness is one of the reasons why relationships in our society today are so shaky. Whenever we gossip, stereotype others unfairly, sulk, apportion blame, let bitterness take over our relationships or talk the language of hate, we have rejected forgiveness and have instead opted for 'preferring darkness to light'. To choose this as a lifestyle option is to lose our humanity, to choose death instead of life.

The runaway son

One of the most powerful stories Jesus ever told was about this issue. Many of his stories seem to be about family relationships or ordinary events but can be read on two levels. Usually we find that Jesus was actually talking about God's relationship to us but in putting them in a story format, he ensured that we would find them easier to understand.

The story of the runaway starts with a son who is bored with life on the farm and asks his father whether he can have his inheritance early so that he can go away and have a good time. He only has one older brother so the father divides the estate – which must have meant selling quite a bit of it – and the son disappears. Quite apart from leaving everybody in the lurch, asking for his inheritance early would have been seen by others at the time as wishing his father dead. The younger son comes over as selfish and self-obsessed. He is also a hedonist. He travels a long way from home and seems to be the 'sex, drugs and rock 'n roll' type. His money is spent on wild parties, booze and prostitutes. He has a lot of friends. However, his money eventually runs out and he wakes up friendless, homeless and increasingly homesick. He ends up looking after pigs and eating their food. The story then says that 'he came to his senses'.

> **If we burn ourselves out with drugs or alcohol, we won't have long to go in this business.**
> *John Belushi*

He quickly realises that even the servants back at home are better off than he is and so decides to throw himself on his father's mercy, asking him to make him a servant, thinking that he's blown it as far as being a son is concerned.

He returns home in a grim state, with his clothes in tatters. It is here that the story shifts to his remarkable father. Seeing him in the distance, the father runs to greet and embrace him. Even before he has heard what his son is trying to tell him about becoming a servant, his father has given him a new ring, a new set of clothes and held a party to celebrate the return of his son from the dead.

The story tells us that the father had been looking out for his son at the gate ever since he had left. After all that time, the father was still expectant. He had received what amounted to a slap in the face from his son, but this did not stop him from loving him. The offer of forgiveness was there waiting, day in and day out. The son did not even have to say sorry, as the father was so overjoyed by his return that he welcomed him back without condition.

His older brother, however, immediately became uncommunicative and full of fury, asking his father why, since he had never left him, he had never been given a party. Why throw one for his wayward son when he had squandered his inheritance? 'Ah,' his father said, 'you are always with me but my other son was dead but now is alive.' Presumably, not a very satisfactory answer for the elder brother!

> **How great is the love the Father
> has lavished on us, that we should
> be called children of God! And that
> is what we are!**
> *1 John 3:1*

Treating God badly

The story is, of course, really about God, the father, and us, the runaway child. The Bible says that we have been given life itself by God but have ignored him. Instead, we have gone our own way and lived our lives without any reference to God. We might see a need to ask for forgiveness from each other but we cannot see that even if

God existed, there would be any need to ask for or receive forgiveness from him. Have we done anything to offend, hurt or abuse God? Surely not.

The Christian faith revolves around the love of God. It suggests that God loves us to such an extent that all human love is a pale imitation by comparison. Our love is a doodle compared to God's Rembrandt. From the very beginning, we were made for a relationship with God. We are not just emotional or sexual people but also spiritual and that dimension is to serve as a reminder that we can have a relationship with God. Just as we have been made a unique person, so we are made to have a unique relationship with God.

If that is so, however, then things have gone pretty badly wrong. Human history shows that we have treated God as a person whom we sometimes fear, often try to manipulate, and occasionally love, but usually only when it suits us. Largely, however, we are just indifferent or even hostile. If God were our partner, then we would have been unfaithful time and time again. Surely he is fed up with us by now and wants to leave us?

The story of the runaway son, however, says not. Whatever lies the son was telling his friends at his parties, however badly he behaved night after night, the father was patiently waiting at the gate looking and longing for the return of the one who had abused him and who had turned his back on him. He had rebelled against all the values and standards of his upbringing and yet when defeated, he returned to the loving embrace of his father and was immediately forgiven.

I believe that this is the great truth that lies at the heart of the Christian faith. It is about returning to the father, accepting God's offer of forgiveness and learning to live as a member of the family again with all that entails. The offer of forgiveness is there 24/7 but it must be accepted if its liberating power is going to lift the burdens of the past and wipe the slate clean. It is unconditionally offered to us but by accepting it, we acknowledge that we need it.

The cost of that forgiveness was the death of Christ on the cross. The Bible tells us that this death was unjust in that he had done nothing wrong on two counts. First, he was there on trumped-up charges, serving ulterior motives of wicked and scheming religious leaders. Secondly, the Bible tells us that the death of Jesus was something that he did for us. In other words, although we have done wrong through our sin and have brought death into the world as a result, Jesus played no part in this. But by dying when he could have gone back to the Father without death, he stood alongside us in our human failings. In fact, he went further than mere identification with us, as unnecessary as this was. He died instead of us.

I remember a war film that was set in a concentration camp within Asia. The soldiers were treated harshly and life was cheap. On one occasion, they all had to line up and were told that a shovel had been stolen. The guilty person was asked to step forward, the implication being that he would be killed for his crime. No one initially owned up but then someone stepped forward. He was brutally murdered. Later they discovered that he was innocent as they had miscounted the number of shovels. He had been prepared to die so that the guilty person might live.

Christians believe that Jesus died so that we might live and, in rising from the dead, defeated death itself and enabled all those who believe in him to see death as a door to a new world rather than the end of all things. When Jesus said, on the cross, 'Father, forgive them because they do not know what they are doing,' he was of course referring to those who had nailed him to the cross. But he was also talking about you and me. Because I believe that it was all of humanity that put him there, including you and me; our wrongdoing that ensured he had to die. There is no greater act of forgiveness than that.

The runaway son story initially states that forgiveness is for losers but we can only appreciate what that means when we begin to understand what we have lost by ignoring God and being indifferent to his love. When we look at the death of Jesus, it should have been so unnecessary but because of you and me, it became inevitable if the world was to be liberated and renewed.

> **As long as I keep running about asking: 'Do you love me? Do you really love me?' I give all power to the voices of the world and put myself in bondage because the world is filled with 'ifs'. The world says: 'Yes, I love you if you are good-looking, intelligent, and wealthy. I love you if you have a good education, a good job, and good connections. I love you if you produce much, sell much, and buy much.'**
> *Henri Nouwen*

10 No such thing as 'quite unique'

Christians believe that Jesus is unique. All history before him looked forward to his coming. All history after him looks back to his life. All history to come looks forward to his return. He is the fulcrum through which human history turns and the person through whom all human history can be understood. History is his story.

Not just a nice guy then.

'Unique' is a word that cannot be qualified. There is no such thing as 'very unique', or 'most unique', or even 'perfectly unique'. If something is unique then there is nothing else like it.

> **Our city's most unique restaurant is now even more unique.**
> *Advertising slogan*

The claim by Christians that Jesus is unique is therefore quite startling. It is not the same as saying that you and I are unique because nobody else has our personality or looks. On the face of it, Christianity's claim seems a little over the top. It claims that Jesus is both God and human. But that being God is not compromised by being human and being human is not compromised by being God. So

Jesus went through the experiences we go through, both good and bad, and felt them just as keenly as we do. Yet he never did anything wrong. He was the perfect human being.

Christians say that if we want to know what it means to be human, then we should look at Jesus. He is the model for all of us. And yet despite the fact that he was human, he was able to heal, forgive sin and perform miracles, the greatest of which was his own resurrection. Two billion people in a world of 6 billion believe this. Why? What is this uniqueness for?

What do Christians believe about the idea of having a relationship with God? The phrase is bandied about a great deal and can quickly become a cliché. Once again it is based on the idea of costly forgiveness. Those who were against Jesus during his life believed that only God could forgive sins. Jesus repeatedly told people that their sins were forgiven. But how could a mere man do this?

I certainly don't have the right or the power to say that your sins are forgiven. I can say that I forgive you for what you have done wrong to me. But what I cannot say is that I forgive you for what you might have done wrong in the eyes of God. And yet Jesus did just that. Over and over again he said, 'your sins are forgiven.' How could Jesus intervene without making an audacious claim to be God? His critics saw this as blasphemy and it was one of the things that led to his crucifixion.

But for those who believe that Jesus is God, this lifting of the burden of past wrongs and the wiping of the slate clean prepares the way for a new relationship, not with another person of equal status, but with God himself. This is not just a matter of intellectual belief. It takes us beyond that into the realm of a relationship with a person who, though they are invisible, loves us unconditionally.

For Christians, accepting this forgiveness ensures that we can go beyond forgiveness to reconciliation. Just as forgiveness can be a one-way process because it is not accepted by the person being offered it, reconciliation is mutual. It establishes a new relationship between two people.

> **You will know the truth, and the truth will set you free.**
> *Jesus*

Telling the truth

In South Africa during the long period of apartheid, the vast majority of people were oppressed by white supremacist rule with many being murdered in the process. Afterwards, through the influence of people such as Archbishop Desmond Tutu, a Truth and Reconciliation Commission was set up in order to bring people together in acts of forgiveness. Indeed, the aim was to go beyond forgiveness to reconciliation, which involved both parties agreeing to put the past behind them. However, it was important for the truth to be told before reconciliation could take place and many who had taken part in violent and unjust practices under the previous regime found it impossible to come forward in order to take advantage of the amnesty that was on offer.

Similarly, truth-telling is at the heart of the Christian faith. First, because it is impossible to receive forgiveness unless you know what that forgiveness is for. Secondly, if reconciliation is going to take place it must be done through facing up to the past and agreeing that although you cannot forget what has happened in the past, it will never affect your relationship again and will never be brought up. A relationship can only survive if truth is at the heart of it and as there are no secrets from God anyway, we are deluding ourselves if we attempt to keep them.

> **I believe in Christianity as I believe that the sun has risen: not only because I see it, but because by it I see everything else.**
> C. S. Lewis

The Old Testament prophet Isaiah represented God when he said, 'I, even I, am he who blots out your transgression for my own sake, and remembers your sins no more' (Isaiah 43:25).

Today, the language may seem archaic, the word 'transgression' meaning 'wrongdoing', but the idea remains powerful. When forgiveness and reconciliation occur, God deliberately decides that the things we have done wrong in the past need not be mentioned ever again. They will not be brought up at any point in the future. They are forgiven. The slate is wiped clean. This doesn't mean that we don't sometimes have to go to other people and put things right, which can sometimes be painful or even embarrassing, but it does mean that we are liberated from a guilty conscience and from trying to hide 'Gollum-like' from God. This ensures not only are we forgiven and benefit from being reconciled but that we are also being transformed. In other words, we are becoming more like the person we most admire and seek to emulate, Jesus.

This is a lifelong journey, however, and one in which we will have many mishaps. It will be fuelled by longing, not only that we would become more like Jesus but also that this world would become a better world.

As we have seen, we live in the midst of poverty and pain as well as beauty and celebration. And yet the Bible tells us that there is a new world coming, where poverty, disability, injustice and evil will be no more.

This is an actual world, not a cloudy and vague 'heaven'. One where there is creativity, love, friendship and a world bursting with new environmental energy. The apostle Paul gives us the wonderful metaphor of our world groaning like a woman wanting to give birth to the next world.

No wonder we long for justice. No wonder all longing is at the heart of spirituality. No wonder we are dissatisfied with what is served up politically in our society or horrified at what is happening environmentally. All of that longing is a longing for the new world to come. This world seems to be fatally compromised and although we must work for its transformation and for justice, I believe that it will always be flawed until the new world comes.

The kingdom of God

When Jesus was healing people, befriending those who were outcasts and talking about his idea of 'the kingdom of God', he was giving us a glimpse of what this new world will be like. He could only heal a few but he showed that the new world would be without disability. He could only encourage a few of the spiritually humble who were often materially poor but, in doing so, showed that it was they and not the self-righteous rich who would be at the heart of his new world.

At the moment, all those who follow him try to live according to the principles he laid down, knowing that although this new world has not yet come and that therefore Jesus' kingdom is invisible, one day we shall live in a world as concrete as this one but at the heart of which will be Jesus and all that he stands for.

We have now passed through four phases of a journey that started at the beginning of this book: creation, that we are made in the image of God and that the world was pronounced 'good'; compromise, that all of us have to come to terms with the dark side of our lives, realising that even the environment is affected by sin and evil; reconciliation, that God offers to forgive us and restore our relationship and the new world, that we look forward to with renewed hope.

> **Jesus says, 'I love you the way you are, and I love you too much to let you stay the way you are.'**
> *Chris Lyons*

But, if we don't have a thorough view of creation, we will not be able to understand God's original intentions or see the essential goodness in each human being. If we don't have a thorough view of the compromise and darkness of the world in which we include ourselves, we will not be realistic about who we are and what we can do as human beings and realise just how much we have resisted God. If we don't have a thorough appreciation of reconciliation, especially the way in which Jesus offers us forgiveness, we cannot understand just how far it is possible to be changed by God as we follow Jesus. And if we don't have a thorough view of the new world, we will have an inadequate hope for the future. We will not know where we are heading.

Christians believe that Jesus, through his resurrection, waits for us in this new world and that we are therefore pilgrims heading towards a known destination.

However, there is one problem and it is not a small one either. We live in an age where all religions, and indeed worldviews, are said to be equal. Whether it is 'new age' beliefs about crystal healing or the ideas of other religions, the spirit of the age rests on the principle that truth is what you make it. No one religion has the right to say that it is true and the others are not, we are told.

If I came up to you and tried to tell you that the Christian faith is true for you regardless of whether you believe it, you might ask, 'what right do you have to say that what you believe is also true for me? It may be true for you. That's great. But to say it is true for me is arrogant.' The Manic Street Preachers 1998 album was called *This is my truth, tell me yours*. Truth today has become personal. It's not something that we necessarily share in common. It's become private rather than public, subjective rather than objective.

The Uniqueness of Jesus

Herein lies the problem. Christians cannot stand back from claiming that Jesus uniquely shows us who God is. His claim, 'I am the way and the truth and the life. No one comes to the Father except through me' (John 14:6) is perhaps the clearest indication we have that he believed that he was not just a prophet or a good teacher. He believed himself to be unique. Uniquely God. Uniquely man. Uniquely able to show us God.

So it's not just the beliefs of Christians that are confident in the extreme. One of the choices we have to make is over the beliefs of Jesus about himself. It's not so much that we have found the truth and want to persuade others of it although that is true. It's more that we have found someone who claims to be the truth and are learning to live in the light of that. This does not mean that we should not respect other beliefs and affirm all that we can agree on together. But it does mean that at some point we will part company with those who don't believe in the uniqueness of Jesus. The problem is that this is offensive to quite a lot of people but Christians would not be true to themselves if they pretended otherwise.

> **Christianity, if false, is of no importance, and if true, of infinite importance. The only thing it cannot be is moderately important.**
> C. S. Lewis

So what are you going to do about Jesus? Do you admire him and want to follow him? Are you indifferent and don't understand what the fuss is all about? Do you think he's not worth bothering with and simply want to walk away? Jesus is in the dock. You decide.

Perhaps it's the idea of getting together with other Christians that puts you off. After all, according to the media, Christians are meant to be a pretty unattractive bunch. However, I've found the opposite. Follow any cause, whether it is football or politics, and people want to share their enthusiasm with others. It's the same with Christianity where many of us would like to find others with whom we can learn more about our faith and discover people with whom we can pray.

At other times we might want to take social or political action about some issue that we feel is unjust. On other occasions we might want to open our heart to somebody over things that have gone wrong in our life. We want to live in a culture of praise. We want to know what it means to worship. We want somewhere to sing without joining a choir. And above all, we want to love and be loved, not least by God.

Of course, there are still hypocrites around. There are in any movement. Even atheists may find themselves praying when their car is heading towards a wall at a rapid rate, or their child dying before their eyes. Hypocrisy is not just about religion; it's about 'do as I say not as I do'.

We're getting near to the end of this book now. So far the message has been that you are an amazing person. OK, you are flawed. But you can make a real difference in this world. There are things that you can do which will make a real impact. You can make a mark on the world that no one else can make. The best way to do this is to rediscover who you are, and to do that I believe you have to rediscover the love of God as revealed through the life of Jesus. In the last chapter, we'll look at the implications of this for the way you live your life.

Following the deep channel

11

When in the movie *Harry Potter and the Goblet of Fire* Professor Dumbledore contrasted what is right and what is easy, he spoke wisely. This book has been about such a tension in two ways. First, we must grapple with some of the key issues that face us as a generation and believe that we can make a difference even though the world is complex and any answers to the problems may, at first, seem out of reach. Secondly, we need to ask what kind of person we should be and what path we ought to follow in order to be spiritually whole.

> **The fishermen know that the sea is dangerous and the storm terrible, but they have never found those dangers sufficient reason for remaining ashore.**
> *Vincent Van Gogh*

Taking the easy path does not use up much energy. It does not require courage or character or a vision in life. We can pin our hopes on a lottery ticket and sink our dreams in a pint of beer. We can even go on exciting trips to exotic places, build environmentally sound houses, read Shakespeare before breakfast and generally be an interesting OK person but still be spiritually numb. It is only when disaster strikes that we realise that we have no roots planted in anything with any substance. We are not, as King David writing in the Psalms puts it, 'like a tree planted by streams of water,' living out a fruitful life.

Those people who followed Jesus while he was alive had no idea where they were going until near the end of his time on earth. It was only then that they realised they were following a man who was going to his death and that they might end up dying with him. Before this point, at least some of them had thought that they were following somebody who was going to liberate Israel from Roman occupation. The point for them then was not so much where they were going but who they were with. Peter, one of his closest and most trusted followers, said when the the time for Jesus' death drew near, 'I will lay down my life for you.' He did, crucified many years later for his belief in Jesus, but not before he had denied any knowledge of Jesus three times when asked, albeit in admittedly difficult and risky circumstances.

> **Alexander, Caesar, Charlemagne, and I have founded empires. But on what did we rest the creations of our genius? Upon force. Jesus Christ founded his empire upon love, and at this hour millions of men would die for him.**
> *Napoleon Bonaparte*

Those who followed Jesus felt a tension between being deeply committed to him and being unsure of the consequences of such a commitment. And yet a few weeks after his death, they became fearless, willing to stand up to the most hostile authorities in order to tell them about the uniqueness of Jesus Christ and his implications for the world. They were with a man who spent his whole life giving away whatever he had to other people: time, power, money, love, privacy and life itself. His teaching was that it was only the people who could give away their life that would then truly find it.

One of the writers of the New Testament gospels, Luke, quotes Jesus as saying: 'If anyone would come after me, he must deny himself and take up his cross daily and follow me. For whoever wants to save his life will lose it, but whoever loses his life for me will save it.'

Secure enough to serve others

Live life for yourself and it shrinks before your eyes. Give it away to other people and it blossoms in all directions. In particular, give it away to God and accept what God gives back in return. You may be surprised. One of the great passages in the Bible about this describes Jesus washing his disciples' dirty feet before a meal (John 13:1–17). This was usually the job of the lowest servant but Jesus insisted on doing it, although Peter tried to.

Before it happened, the Bible says that Jesus would do this knowing that it was one of the last things he would do in order to show them how much he loved them. The Bible deliberately says that before he performed this menial task, Jesus was aware that he was all-powerful:

- He had come from God: his origins
- He was returning to God: his destiny
- He knew who he was: his identity.

Because he was secure in these three things, he could

lay down his power to help others. Because he knew that he was the Son of God, he was set free to be a servant.

The same is true of us. When we are secure in our origins (made in the image of God), our destiny (pilgrims heading towards a new world) and our identity (modelling our lives on Jesus), then we can be set free to serve others. The question is whether we are ready to take on that identity.

In an earlier chapter, I talked about being careful in what we are ambitious for. There is nothing wrong with ambition per se but if we put our trust and energy in the wrong things, then we can be blinded to the real purpose of life. Ambition which is limited to material goals for our own lives may give us a visible path and sharply defined goals. What it does not tell us is what kind of person we will end up being when we get there.

What is needed are more people who will be other-person focused and who will grapple with the issues of the day because they believe that the world can be a better place than it is now. In other words, what is needed are people who are so committed that the word 'ambitious' is too weak for them, utterly dedicated as they are to transforming the world and, in the same way as the mosquito has an impact inordinate for its size, believe that even one person can change the world. I believe that God is at the heart of that transformation.

Living for others puts those who are worse off than ourselves in sharp focus. It requires us to examine ourselves and the way that we live. Christians have to live with the words of the Old Testament prophet Micah, 'he has showed you, O man, what is good. And what does the Lord require of you? To act justly and to love mercy and to walk humbly with your God' (Micah 6:8). It suggests that we are people who are not called just to be passionate about justice, or to act mercifully towards those who may wrong us, but also, be people who walk humbly with God, knowing that it is only down that path that we will find the very best for our lives. It is not where we are going so much as who we are travelling with.

Heading out to sea

Writers seldom have anything that they can call a career and I remember talking about this to a friend of mine who had become an eminent doctor. He told me the following story.

An oil tanker leaves a harbour bound for another port. As it goes out to sea, it turns away from its destination and sails for many miles, then it turns and takes off in seemingly the wrong direction again. It seems to be doing anything but head for its destination. Why? It is following the deep channel. Any other direction and its hull would be grounded because the water is too shallow for the enormous ship.

> **Greatness is not in where we stand but in what direction we are moving. We must sail sometimes with the wind and sometimes against it – but sail we must and not drift, not lie at anchor.**
> Oliver Wendell Holmes

The person who is following Jesus and desires nothing more than what God wants for them cannot assume that their life will go from A to Z with no detours. There may be setbacks and pain or unexpected joy and celebration. What is important is to follow the deep channel even if everything in our society seems to scream the exact opposite.

We have an occasional ritual in our family when a 'deep and meaningful' discussion threatens to become heated for no real reason. Somebody will step in and say, 'keep it shallow'. Usually it is enough to cause a smile to creep up on the most heated members of the family. But if our aim in life is to always 'keep it shallow', we will miss out not only on what it means to be human but also in not contributing to the lives of other people across the world that we could have touched and helped had we been willing to take a risk and reach out to them.

It's easy to paddle in the shallows. It's risky to sail out to sea. But that's where God is. If we want to be filled with God, if we want our life to remind others of the life of Jesus. If we just want our life to count for something, then we need to push our boat out and sail.

To follow the deep channel.